The Novels of Jane Austen

THE NOVELS OF

Jane Austen

Robert Liddell

LONGMANS

LONGMANS, GREEN AND CO. LTD
London and Harlow
*Associated companies, branches and representatives
throughout the world*

PRINTED AND BOUND IN ENGLAND BY
HAZELL WATSON AND VINEY LTD
AYLESBURY, BUCKS

To Ivy Compton-Burnett

Contents

Abbreviations

The following abbreviations are used.

JANE AUSTEN'S WORKS

N. A. *Northanger Abbey*   M. P. *Mansfield Park*
S. S. *Sense and Sensibility*   E.   *Emma*
P. P. *Pride and Prejudice*   P.   *Persuasion*
               M. W. *Minor Works*

Letters Jane Austen's Letters to her sister Cassandra and others, collected and edited by R. W. Chapman, 2nd edit. 1952

All quotations from the novels are from Dr Chapman's edition; double inverted commas indicate direct speech. The Letters are referred to by their numbers in Dr Chapman's edition.

OTHER WORKS FREQUENTLY CITED

Memoir Memoir of Jane Austen, by her nephew James Edward Austen-Leigh, ed. R. W. Chapman (Oxford, 1926).

Life Jane Austen, her life and letters, a family record by William Austen-Leigh and Richard Arthur Austen-Leigh (London, 1913).

Lascelles Jane Austen and her Art, by Mary Lascelles (Oxford, 1939).

Leavis A Critical Theory of Jane Austen's Writings, by Q. D. Leavis (Scrutiny X, 1, 2, 3, 1941–2).

Chapman Jane Austen: Facts and Problems (Oxford, 1948).

Apology

A new book on Jane Austen may appear to require some apology; it has, however, seemed to me for some years that such a thing was wanted.

The serious criticism of Jane Austen has lately suffered from separatism, as biographical studies of this author suffered in the last century. Then the Austen-Leighs seem to have had little contact with the Austen-Knights, and it was not until the *Life* (1913) that all the documents were put together, and the Kentish and Hampshire parts of the author's experience were welded into a whole. In this century (though Dr Chapman's careful scholarship must be the basis of any intelligent work on Jane Austen) Oxford and Cambridge critics have been too little aware each of the others' work.

The admirable book by Miss Mary Lascelles (1939) is completely ignored by Mrs Leavis in her remarkable articles (1941-2); and these articles are not mentioned by Dr Chapman in his Clark lectures (1948), though they raise precisely the sort of 'Facts and Problems' upon which we should particularly have valued his opinion. A student who begins by making a synthesis of what these writers tell us, will probably find that he is tempted to go on further in several directions, where they have pointed the way. Such was the genesis of this book: I have also (I think) made a number of small discoveries which I have not yet seen anywhere in print, and which it seemed worth recording for the pleasure and profit of other readers. In short, the following pages must be their own justification.

It is not to be supposed that I shall succeed, where the above-mentioned writers and others have failed, in destroying the popular myth of Jane Austen. She was not the inspired amateur who (almost by divine inspiration) dashed off novels between household tasks; she did not write the three 'Steventon' novels between the ages of twenty-one and twenty-three; she did not have eight to ten 'silent years', and then suddenly write the three 'Chawton' novels; it is not true that no development can be traced in her work. Other people (notably Mrs Leavis) have completely proved the falsity of this myth, and in the following pages (especially in the first section devoted to each novel) I shall restate the evidence.

Jane Austen would, no doubt, have liked to start life as a young author, like Fanny Burney. Very fortunately her early drafts of novels were unsuccessful with publishers: *First Impressions* was rejected unseen, *Susan* languished in a cupboard or a drawer. Late nineteenth century and other admirers have exclaimed at those publishers' stupidity, but, very likely, these works were then jejune and unformed; their premature

xi

publication might have robbed us forever of the author whom we know, the slow developer, the patient and creative reviser, whose writing life extended from schoolroom days until her last illness, and whose genius lay, for the most part, in taking pains.

Jane Austen is often, and very ineptly, compared with Shakespeare; it is hard to see how anyone who sincerely admired either of them could make that comparison, or could suppose that they were trying to do the same thing. His handling of character and intrigue is often no more impressive than her verbal poetry. But their fate has in some ways been similar: they are standard and accepted authors, as no other English author is, and people think they have a knowledge of them that is almost 'infused', and feel able to write about them without previous study, in a way in which no one would venture to write about Milton or George Eliot. When these people (as it sometimes happens) are critics or scholars of distinction in other fields, or when their misguided remarks appear (as they sometimes do) under the *imprimatur* of a learned body, or a respectable periodical, this is a pity. The serious student of Jane Austen is obliged to push this rubbish on one side (which is a waste of his time), and he must try to do so with suavity; no writing about this author ought to be arrogant, pompous or ill-tempered.

It is therefore with reluctance that I find myself obliged to make an example of Mr Edmund Wilson, one of the most distinguished critics of our time.

It is true that he was reviewing a book, a simple, chatty, but not unlikeable book by two devout worshippers of Jane Austen; nevertheless, he allowed his article to be collected and printed. Although he paid tribute to Mrs Leavis's articles (which, naturally, he thought were on an entirely different level of seriousness), he seems completely to have missed or forgotten their point, for he goes on to say (in his own 'comments'): 'The half-dozen novels of Jane Austen were written in two sets of three each, with an interval of about ten years between the two.' He complains that the two ladies whom he is reviewing thought of the six novels as always co-existing; if they did, they were a little nearer the truth than he.

He then gives us his opinion on *Mansfield Park*, which he says he has not read for thirty years. It is a complex and difficult book, and if he had read it once in each of those thirty years, we should have been grateful for Mr Wilson's help towards understanding it.

And then (though Mr Wilson rejects the adjective 'Freudian'), it seems to the reader that Freud raises his ugly head. We are told of the 'big sister' and her authority, over Marianne Dashwood and Elizabeth Bennet, and we are invited to believe in a 'false-sister' relationship between Harriet and Emma, and between Anne Elliot and Lady Russell. It is suggested that Mr Knightley will not be very happy in his marriage, as Emma will insist on bringing another protegée into the house. 'Emma,' he writes, 'who was relatively indifferent to men, was inclined to infatuations with women.'

When Mr Wilson provided a 'Freudian' explanation of *The Turn of the Screw*, I (so I think) disproved it.[1] His theory of Jane Austen I may leave to be rejected out of hand by anyone who has read the novels rather more recently.

This sort of irresponsible writing shows the need to set the criticism of this writer on a surer basis. Another nuisance, that must be cleared out of the way, is the 'social' criticism of her work.

It is complained that she wrote only about the upper middle class. As this was the class that she knew, her restraint is commendable: the excursions of Hardy and of Henry James into worlds that they imperfectly understood were not very successful. A reader who is not hysterically class-conscious will take characters as people, and their life as life, without much caring about their social level. Elizabeth Bennet and Bérénice interest us as human beings, and we should not care that one is a queen and the other a gentleman's daughter, were it not that their state of life affects their destinies.

Those who object that she was indifferent to the lot of the 'lower orders' may (if they choose) learn from the excellent biography by Miss Elizabeth Jenkins that they are very much mistaken. This is a matter of biographical fact and, as such, was part of Miss Jenkins's province, and she has admirably dealt with it. We may all, who love her, be glad that Jane Austen's attitude was liberal and humane. But as critics of her work we are not at all concerned with her attitude to a subject which she has not chosen to treat. And (though faults of omission are, of course, possible to them) it is always highly temerarious to blame artists for not treating this or that subject; you have (unless you are proceeding on a vicious theory) to prove that they were *artistically* obliged to treat the subject in question.

More tiresome is that kind of criticism which accuses her of too great a preoccupation with social minutiae, for it is near enough to the truth to require an answer, and such an answer cannot be given without a dwelling on the subject that may be tedious to some readers. I will not aggravate their tedium by saying more of it here, except to remark that, when discussing an author who is for all time, one must feel some impatience at having to linger over accidents of class and time and place. Nevertheless, these things must be put in their proper perspective, or she may be misunderstood.

As for the blind worshippers of this writer, I must appeal to them to follow me with patience to the end. If I seek (as every responsible critic

[1] *A Treatise on the Novel*, pp. 138–145.

has for some time sought) to destroy the popular (and, alas, probably indestructible) ikon of Jane Austen, it is only in order to make room for one that more nearly corresponds with the truth, and is more to be admired. If I see traces of crude early work in *Pride and Prejudice*, and find unresolved difficulties in *Mansfield Park*, most people would say the same of *Hamlet*. If I believe *Persuasion* is unfinished, we know that the same thing is true of *Hyperion* and of Beauvais cathedral. I can only say that my own deep admiration of this writer has been further deepened by making this study, and that I do not believe any critic has yet given her higher praise than I have. I hope to have added something to the enjoyment that a few readers may derive from her work, and I cannot imagine that I can have spoiled anyone's pleasure in it.

For some people, Jane Austen's novels will always be what the Baronetage was to Sir Walter Elliot: 'occupation for an idle hour, and consolation in a distressed one'. I cannot think she would resent this use of her books. People are so unfortunate, that no right-feeling author will be displeased at giving them some comfort—people are so wicked, that an author may, at the lowest, feel some satisfaction in keeping them innocently occupied for a few hours in the perusal of his work. I should not wish to snatch *Emma* or *Mansfield Park* from anyone who was comfortably cushioned upon it, and momentarily protected by it from the sharp corners of life; but I would suggest a nobler use for it. Through good and evil days this writer can prop our mind, and her works can be our rod and staff.

Northanger Abbey

§1. Its History

According to Cassandra Austen's note[1] 'it was written in 1797 and 1798', that is, after *First Impressions* and *Sense and Sensibility* (or concurrently with the latter). Mrs Leavis[2] conjectured that it was 'probably written up from an unfinished story in *Volume the Third* called 'Catherine, or the Bower'. This conjecture (made before the publication of that story) can hardly now be accepted, though some traits of the unheroic Catherine may indeed have been transferred to Catherine Morland.

It is almost certain that this was (or was an early draft of) the 'MS novel in two vols., entitled *Susan*', which was sold in the spring of 1803 to Messrs. Crosby and Co. of Stationers' Hall Court for £10.[3] In the 'Advertisement by the Authoress' it is said to have been 'finished' in that year, which implies rewriting at the time when Jane Austen was living in Bath.

In April 1809 Jane Austen wrote (probably from Southampton) to Crosby to enquire why no publication had taken place, and to supply another copy if necessary, though unable 'from particular circumstances to command this copy before the month of August',[4] when she would be settled at Chawton. Crosby replied that she might have the MS back for £10.

'One of her brothers' (presumably Henry) bought it back after the publication of *Emma*; after the publisher had concluded the bargain, 'the negotiator had the satisfaction of informing him that the work which had been so lightly esteemed was by the author of "Pride and Prejudice" '.[5] Jane Austen bought back the copyright with the idea of making some use of it, and the Advertisement shows that the book was prepared for the press in 1816; but it seems that she had been unable to revise it in a way to satisfy her, for, in March 1817, she wrote to Fanny Knight: 'Miss Catherine is put upon the Shelve for the present, and I do not know that she will ever come out. . . .'[6] It was published in 1818, after her death, together with *Persuasion*.

It is therefore a book which had been being written during most of her adult life. Dr Chapman's 'chronology'[7] establishes a probability that she used the calendar of 1798 for its construction; if so, the main story must have been fixed at that date. We cannot now know how much work was done on it when it was prepared for the press in 1803. Miss Lascelles[8] gives us reasons for supposing that the passage defending novels and their readers is an answer to Maria Edgeworth's condemnation in the 'advertisement' to *Belinda* (1801).

When the MS went to Crosby, a duplicate evidently remained in the author's hands, and she may have worked on it from time to time; possibly another revision was undertaken in 1809, when she made a second attempt to secure publication; both Dr Chapman[9] and Mrs Leavis[10] favour this date. At all events, by 1817, it had turned from 'Susan' to 'Miss Catherine'—a change which the author would hardly trouble to make unless a very complete revision gave her the opportunity.

The 'Advertisement' certainly indicates that she had not bothered to bring it up-to-date: 'The public are entreated to bear in mind that thirteen years have passed since it was finished, many more since it was begun, and that during that period, places, manners, books and opinions have undergone considerable changes.' This does not, however, forbid us to think that no changes of style or tone had been made since 1803.

It is perhaps noteworthy that, in her letter to Crosby in April 1809, Jane Austen does not insist on replacing his copy by a revised version; but in her letter she is only feeling the way, and we cannot tell what she might have proposed had the negotiations continued.

The only legitimate conclusion is that hardly any part of the book can be securely dated.

§2. Burlesque and Imitation

It is probably the truth that this, more than any other of this writer's novels, illustrates an early phase of her work, despite the revisions which it has undergone. The recalcitrant story, which Jane Austen was evidently unable to bring into a form that satisfied her before she died, is one indication of this; another is the large and overt part given to burlesque, which connects this book with the early parodies.

It has no doubt been said (and it would no doubt be true to say)

2

that Jane Austen began this story of an anti-heroine in a pure spirit of parody, and then became interested in her characters as Fielding became interested in those of *Joseph Andrews*. It is impossible (as we have seen) to say how slowly this change came about, or through how many recensions. Finally, it is a minor work of art, a criticism of both art and life—the two integrated, so that life criticizes literature—but one unrealized and purely functional character, and an ineradicable weakness in the original plot, prevented the author from bringing the book to full maturity.

Miss Lascelles[11] admirably analyses the skill with which Jane Austen uses one mouthpiece after another to state 'the laws of fiction', and to point out to the heroine the differences between life and art; and I am much indebted to her discussion.

At first it is the author who speaks, stating the disqualifications of Catherine Morland as a heroine.

Her parentage is against her. 'Her father was a clergyman, without being neglected, or poor, and a very respectable man, though his name was Richard.'[12] This is a family joke (cf. 'Mr Richard Harvey's match is put off till he has got a Better Christian Name, of which he has great Hopes.')[13] Catherine's mother did not die at her birth, 'as any body' (i.e. any novel reader) might expect; and Catherine grew up with no claim to beauty and less to accomplishment. 'She never could learn or understand anything before she was taught; and sometimes not even then',[14] and even when she was 'improved', the height of her musical powers was to 'listen to other people's performance with very little fatigue'. And as to drawing, she could not 'attempt a sketch of her lover's profile, that she might be detected in the design',[15] even if she had had a lover. Her inferiority in 'heroism' is striking when compared (as Miss Lascelles compares it)[16] with that of Emmeline, eponymous heroine of Charlotte Smith's novel,[17] who had 'made herself mistress without any instruction' of most accomplishments; who 'had learned to play on the harp, by being present when Mrs Ashwood received lessons on that instrument', and with almost as little help from masters, was able to execute a faultless portrait of her lover.

Nor has any 'amiable youth' appeared as a hero; Catherine, at seventeen, was heartwhole. 'This was strange indeed! But strange things may be generally accounted for if their cause be fairly searched out. There was not one lord in the neighbourhood; no—

not even a baronet. There was not a family among their acquaintance who had reared and supported a boy accidentally found at their door—not one young man whose origin was unknown. Her father had no ward, and the squire of the parish no children.'[18]

Here the burlesque is of the obvious kind, practised by Fielding and by Dickens; all the world of fiction is its victim; novels of the sentimental and of the 'horror' school, and even the more realistic works of Fanny Burney. But Fanny Burney is also, in another way, an 'influence'. Like Evelina, Catherine is introduced into the world; she accompanies Mr and Mrs Allen, the squire and his wife, on a visit to Bath.

Her departure from home is unheroic. Her mother does not warn her 'against the violence of such noblemen and baronets as delight in forcing young ladies away to some remote farm-house'.[19] Her sister Sarah does not insist 'on Catherine's writing by every post', nor 'transmitting the character of every new acquaintance, nor a detail of every interesting conversation that Bath might produce'[20]—a fine opening for an epistolary novel is thus thrown away.

When the hero, Henry Tilney, appears, he immediately, and with a charming archness, treats Catherine as a heroine, and reminds her of the duties of her state; to begin with, she must, of course, keep a journal.[21]

He is reinforced by the confidante, Isabella Thorpe, who not only reminds Catherine of the 'laws of fiction', but introduces her to a great many new novels. Isabella's oafish brother, John, discommends the novels of Mrs Radcliffe to us, because he finds some 'fun and nature' in them (which is exactly what they lack); and his contempt for Camilla, by 'that woman they made such a fuss about, she who married the French emigrant',[22] is the warmest compliment to Madame d'Arblay. Presently the equally sincere compliment of imitation will again be paid to her Evelina; Catherine is asked to dance by Henry Tilney, and John Thorpe annoys her by insisting that she had a previous engagement with himself.[23]

Catherine, when left without a mentor, continues to play her unheroic role. She sees a young woman with Henry Tilney, and 'throwing away a fair opportunity of considering him lost to her for ever, by being married already', at once concludes that it is his sister.[24] For she is still 'guided only by what was simple and probable'. And when the author dismisses her 'to a pillow strewed with thorns and wet with tears' after a misunderstanding over a walk with the Tilneys,[25] we are not anxious about her; on a previous occasion, disappointment brought on no more tragic consequences than an 'Extraordinary hunger . . . and earnest longing to be in bed', followed by 'a sound sleep which lasted nine hours'.[26]

The confidante, Isabella, now takes the middle of the stage as an affianced bride: "Had I the command of millions, were I mistress of the whole world, your brother would be my only choice."

'This charming sentiment, recommended as much by sense as novelty, gave Catherine a most pleasing remembrance of all the heroines of her acquaintance.'[27]

Catherine, having made friends with the Tilneys, is invited to accompany them home to Gloucestershire, to Northanger Abbey. On the journey, Henry resumes his role as spokesman of the 'laws of fiction'. "Are you prepared to encounter all the horrors that a building such as 'what one reads about' may produce? Have you a stout heart? Nerves fit for sliding panels and tapestry?"[28] He threatens her with a remote and gloomy chamber, with "a ponderous chest which no efforts can open"; to this she is to be escorted by 'Dorothy the ancient housekeeper', who is to be mysteriously struck with her appearance—such (more or less) was the experience of Emily (of *The Mysteries of Udolpho*) when received by Dorothée, the housekeeper at Château le Blanc.

Henry light-heartedly continues his pastiche, proving that his claim to be a novel-addict was no idle boast. A secret door is to be discovered, and (in a small vaulted room within) "a large, old-fashioned cabinet of ebony and gold", and, in "an inner compartment" of this, a roll of paper containing "the memoirs of the wretched Matilda". He knows (as Dr Chapman points out)[29] not only *The Mysteries of Udolpho*, but also *The Romance of the Forest*.

Northanger turns out to be elegant and modernized, nevertheless Catherine's imagination has been aroused, and must be exercised. The large chest in her room is her first temptation (it delays her dressing for dinner): there is nothing in it but 'a white cotton counterpane, properly folded'.[30] Little daunted by this disappointment, she makes an attempt on a 'high, old-fashioned black cabinet'; she is left with a roll of papers in her hand, a carelessly extinguished candle, and a raging storm without. Next day, in the warmth of a fire and the light of a bright morning, she finds that all she has discovered is an old washing-bill. 'She felt humbled to the dust. Could not the adventure of the chest have taught her wisdom?'[31]

It could not. Catherine has wandered too far into the land of Romance, and it is Henry who must lead her back.

General Tilney, who is a very odd (and very ill-drawn) character next awakens her suspicions. He dislikes 'the delightful melancholy'[32] of his late wife's favourite walk; he does not care for her portrait, though 'very like'.[33] He indulges in 'solitary rambles' which 'did not speak a mind at ease, or a conscience void of reproach'.[34] He shrinks from entering Mrs Tilney's room: 'a room in all probability never entered by him since the dreadful scene had passed, which released his suffering wife, and left him to the stings of conscience'.[35]

Eleanor reveals that her mother's last illness was 'sudden and short'. At once Catherine forms the suspicion of murder: 'How many were the examples [in fiction] to justify it!' As the General paced about the drawing-room in the evening, she saw in him 'the air and attitude of a Montoni',[36] the sinister proprietor of the castle of Udolpho. When he stays up, pretexting "many pamphlets to finish", Catherine forms a new idea: 'the probability that Mrs Tilney yet lived, shut up for causes unknown, and receiving from the pitiless hands of her husband a nightly supply of coarse food'.[37] Catherine's surmises are more than reasonable when compared with those indulged by some of her sister heroines.

It does not surprise her that she alone should have guessed the mystery of Northanger, nor that she should be the predestined deliverer of the unhappy captive. At length she penetrates to Mrs Tilney's room—it is a bright, well-furnished, modern room—and at once she is seized by 'bitter emotions of shame'.[38] On retreating, she is caught at the stair-head by Henry, who worms out of her the motives of her curiosity.

He reveals that Mrs Tilney died of nothing more romantic than a bilious fever (like Jane Austen's Bath acquaintance, Marianne Mapleton).[39] "Dear Miss Morland, consider the dreadful nature of the suspicions you have entertained. . . . Consult your own understanding, your own sense of the probable, your own observation of what is passing around you—Does our education prepare us for such atrocities? . . . Could they be perpetrated without being known, in a country like this . . . where every man is surrounded by a neighbourhood of voluntary spies, and where roads and newspapers lay every thing open?''[40] It does not seem to occur to Henry, to Catherine, or to their creator, that he has been partly responsible for Catherine's overheated imagination.

Catherine is now thoroughly awakened, and thoroughly humbled: 'it had all been a voluntary, self-created delusion, each trifling circumstance receiving importance from an imagination resolved on alarm, and every thing forced to bend to one purpose by a mind which, before she entered the Abbey had been craving to be frightened. . . . She saw that the infatuation had been created, the mischief settled long before her quitting Bath, and it seemed as if the whole might be traced to the influence of that sort of reading which she had there indulged.'[41] Catherine decided that Mrs Radcliffe was no guide to human nature, 'at least in the midland counties of England', whatever might happen in the Alps or the Pyrenees, or even in Scotland or Wales.

Hardly had she forgiven herself, and resolved to be very sensible in the future, than a letter from her brother further discredited the world of fiction by revealing the faithlessness of Isabella, her confidante.

Henry puts to her what (as a heroine) should be her feelings on the occasion: "You feel, I suppose, that in losing Isabella, you lose half yourself: you feel a void in your heart which nothing else can occupy. Society is becoming irksome, and as for the amusements in which you were wont to share at Bath, the very idea of them without her is abhorrent. You would not, for instance, now go to a ball for the world. You feel that you have no longer any friend to whom you can speak with unreserve; on whose regard you can place dependence; or whose counsel, in any difficulty, you could rely on. You feel all this?"

Henry, with a mixture of banter and true kindness, is helping her to know herself, and she is able to reply: "I do not feel so very, very much afflicted as one would have thought".[42]

She is now firmly rooted in life, and can place dependence on the young Tilneys, through all the crisis that follows.

*

Burlesque has a second function in this novel; it is not only used in the sentimental education of the heroine, but also (as by Fielding, Thackeray and others) in lighthearted mockery of the novelist's own task, as a technical device to help her over difficulties,

7

and as an ornament applied to disguise weak parts in the construction.

'This brief account of the family is intended to supersede the necessity of a long and minute detail from Mrs Thorpe herself, of her past adventures and sufferings, which might otherwise be expected to occupy the three or four following chapters—in which the worthlessness of lords and attorneys might be set forth; and conversations, which had passed twenty years before, be minutely repeated.'[43]

Here it is well enough, but it will not at all do to explain General Tilney's conduct.

'I leave it to my reader's sagacity to determine how much of all this it was possible for Henry to communicate at this time to Catherine, how much of it he could have learnt from his father, in what points his own conjectures might assist him, and what portion must yet remain to be told in a letter from James. I have united for their ease what they must divide for mine.'[44]

We cannot forget the inadequacy of this, though mollified by Eleanor's marriage to 'the most charming young man in the world'. This is delightful, and outside the story, and the fun is therefore entirely justified. 'Any further definition of his merits must be unnecessary; the most charming young man in the world is instantly before the imagination of us all. Concerning the one in question therefore I have only to add—(aware that the rules of composition forbid the introduction of a character not connected with my fable)—that this was the very gentleman whose negligent servant left behind him that collection of washing-bills. . . .'[45]

§3. The Anti-heroine and the Anti-hero

Catherine, the anti-heroine of romance, is, as Mrs Leavis says, 'launched into the world by an anti-chaperone (for Mrs Allen, like Catherine, is purely functional—hence her concentration on herself and her inability to advise, instruct or watch over her charge'.[46]

Mrs Allen, indeed, cares for little but to be well dressed and to sit still—in which she is the prototype of Lady Bertram in *Mansfield Park*. But I think, in the course of the various recensions of this work, Catherine has outgrown her 'purely functional' character as the unheroic and ordinary girl who enters the world without éclat, falls in love with the hero, and attracts him by her devotion.

As Miss Lascelles says,[47] she has the instincts of a wise child; she may be a goose, but she is not a fool. She is gulled by Isabella, but not quite all the time; she has the shrewdness to perceive her friend's extreme lack of interest in anyone but herself, and the rectitude to feel unhappy at other parts of her conduct. She can invent fantastic nonsense about General Tilney, but she is never deceived about herself as a 'heroine', and she always reacts justly to Henry and Eleanor. She cannot always fully understand them, for at first she does not understand their relations with their father; nevertheless, she will not let Isabella or her own imagination lead her astray over them. She will neither fancy that Henry has fallen in love with her at first sight, nor that he and his sister have treated her with insolence. When she has, herself, been trapped into being rude, she will hasten to make amends and—with a courage that gives her individuality as a 'person'—she can take Henry to task: "But, Mr Tilney, why were *you* less generous than your sister? If she felt such confidence in my good intentions, and could suppose it to be only a mistake, why should *you* be so ready to take offence?"[48] Like so many speeches in Jane Austen's novels, this tells us as much about the person addressed as the speaker; Henry's heart is already affected.

That Catherine was originally conceived as purely functional—whether in 1798 or earlier—one can hardly doubt. But the novel published in 1818 is a blend of life and burlesque, and is nearer to the other novels in the canon than might be thought; there is more parody and burlesque in the later novels and more 'life' in *Northanger Abbey* than is commonly recognized.

The author's purpose would not be achieved if Catherine were a mere doll: it is fit that the anti-heroine should exhibit more life and individuality than the stock heroine, nor, otherwise, could her sentimental education be achieved with such charm and delicacy (the episode of the washing-bills—rightly retained, because it is so amusing—probably dates from a cruder early version, in which Catherine was more roughly made fun of).

Henry falls in love with Catherine: 'a persuasion of her partiality for him had been the only cause of giving her a serious thought. It is a new circumstance in romance, I acknowledge, and dreadfully derogatory of an heroine's dignity; but if it be as new in common life, the credit of a wild imagination will at least be all my own.'[49]

Catherine belongs to common life, and therefore she has to live; Henry 'delighted in all the excellencies of her character and truly loved her society', and we may believe that Jane Austen intended her readers to share in that delight and love.

*

In a different sense from that in which Catherine is the anti-heroine, Henry is like the anti-hero. He is given all the charm that we expect to find in the worthless (or not very worthy) young man who appears in the later novels to trouble the heroine's imagination: Willoughby, Wickham, Henry Crawford, Frank Churchill and even (a slightly older version to tempt an older heroine) William Elliot. Henry has a fluency, a suavity and an address that the 'good' heroes lack: Edward Ferrars, Colonel Brandon, Darcy, Edmund Bertram, Knightley (though Captain Wentworth is not altogether without it). Moreover he is called Henry, a name which Jane Austen particularly liked; it seems to have denoted the exact opposite of Richard, in her mental catalogue of names. It was the name of her favourite brother, and of so many heroes of fiction.[50]

§4. The General

General Tilney is an entirely functional character, whose purpose is to promote the 'distress' of the story. Seeing his younger son paying attention to Catherine, he felt an interest in her; and as he 'like every military man had a very large acquaintance',[51] he was able to apply to John Thorpe for information. John Thorpe, having some expectation of a double marriage between his own family and the Morlands, gave a rosy picture of their fortune and prospects. The General, with simple greed and cunning, decided to cut out John, and to carry Catherine off to Northanger, and groom her as a bride for Henry: an unlikely story that the General should so easily accept the unsupported testimony of John Thorpe; unlikelier, that on a short visit to London some weeks later, he should equally easily believe, on the same testimony, that the Morlands were paupers, and that he should go back in a dudgeon to throw Catherine out of his house.

Such a story would be quite plausible enough for a burlesque of the order of the early parodies, but it could not have satisfied Jane Austen when her art had begun to aspire to a more realistic representation of life.

We have seen the brilliant use made of the General as a pseudo-Montoni, as the imagined murderer or gaoler of his wife; but this, though most beautifully leading to the clarification of Catherine's ideas about life, has no sequel in the development of the plot. She was banished from Northanger on account of the General's illusions, not her own.

Two attempts are made to give him a 'character'.

As a 'flat' character, he is a monster of egoism and vanity, and perfectly unconscious of these faults. He is 'as careless on such subjects' (the size of his dining-room) 'as most people';[52] if he were not 'perfectly without vanity of that kind',[53] he would have ordered new breakfast china of improved manufacture; though 'without any ambition of that sort himself',[54] he believed his gardens unrivalled in the kingdom; 'if he had a vanity, it was in the arrangement of his offices'.[55]

He casts a restraint over his children's spirits, which Catherine cannot at first understand. He is moody, and easily put out by unpunctuality, by any change in his hours (he must take his morning walk early, and professes that it is out of consideration for Catherine's wishes) or by anything less than perfection in his food. In spite of his instructions to Henry to take no particular trouble over his entertainment, his son knows better than to take him at his word, and rides off at once to Woodston to notify his housekeeper. Both Henry and Eleanor are well aware, for all his generous words on the subject to Catherine, that any child of his will be expected to marry money.

To Catherine, he uses the empty and insincere language of compliment from the first: 'saying everything gallant as they went down stairs, admiring the elasticity of her walk, which corresponded exactly with the spirit of her dancing'.[56] Catherine is not critical; she has lately got used to hearing the gush of Isabella Thorpe (though her own purity of speech has not been affected): 'That he was perfectly agreeable and good-natured, and altogether a very charming man, did not admit of a doubt, for he was tall and handsome, and Henry's father'.[57] She does not notice his sycophantic references to the Allens (from whom she is, he hopes, to inherit an estate), or his crude match-making—for example, when he places her in Henry's curricle. (Mrs Grant, in *Mansfield Park*, was to place Julia Bertram on the barouche-box with Henry Crawford; match-making might, indeed, be in her mind, but one feels that she was afraid of Maria occupying that seat, if it were left unassigned.)[58] But Catherine has already turned him into a Montoni in her imagination, before he makes her 'the magnificent compliment': "Can either of us be more meetly employed? *My* eyes will be blinding for the good of others; and *yours* preparing by rest for future mischief."[59] One cannot imagine what good he is going to do anyone by 'poring over the affairs of the nation', but he may not be entirely insincere in thinking that he will; it is no uncommon delusion.

It seems possible that, under cover of the Montoni-like gloom that is to excite Catherine's suspicions, Jane Austen wanted to give the General some redeeming touches of sensibility; he did, in fact, avoid Mrs Tilney's favourite walk and her room. Henry entirely understood that his presence must have prevented Eleanor and Catherine from visiting it. But Henry himself, who is very moderate about 'the domestic, unpretending merits'[60] of his mother, also (and unnecessarily) destroys his father's character for sensibility about her memory: 'His value of her was sincere; and, if not permanently, he was truly afflicted by her death.'[61]

Sense and Sensibility

§1. Its History

Sense and Sensibility, issued in the autumn of 1811, is Jane Austen's first published work. The history of its composition is by no means simple, but if we define what we mean, we may, in a sense, call it her earliest novel.

Cassandra Austen's note of the date of her sister's works is as follows:

> '*First Impressions* (original of *Pride and Prejudice*) begun October 1796, ended August 1797.
> *Sense and Sensibility*, begun November 1797.
> *Northanger Abbey* [probably called *Susan*], written in 1797 and 1798.'[1]

Some critics have asked themselves why Jane Austen chose her second work to publish first.

In fact there is record of an earlier form of *Sense and Sensibility* called *Elinor and Marianne*, which preceded *First Impressions*;[2] her niece, Caroline Austen, records that this novel was 'first written in letters, and *so* read to her family'.[3] The author of the *Memoir* says that the book was begun 'in its present form'[4] in 1797; he probably means that the epistolary *Elinor and Marianne* was then converted into the continuous narrative of *Sense and Sensibility*.

It is therefore likely that the novel which Jane Austen first chose for publication was one that had been both her first full-length book in epistolary form and, subsequently, her first book to be written as a continuous narrative. (The *First Impressions* of 1796–7 was probably still in the form of letters.) It is also likely that considerable revision was done at a later date, before the book was sent to the publishers.

Her brother Henry, who calls her novels 'the gradual performances of her previous life',[5] tells us that 'Though in composition she was equally rapid and correct, yet an invincible distrust of her own judgement induced her to withhold her books from the public, till time and many perusals had satisfied her that the charm of recent composition was dissolved.' He says nothing of continued revision.

The Rev. Henry Austen was not a creative writer, though he wrote 'very superior sermons'; one may, without offence, imagine him re-perusing these with increasing admiration, and attribut-ing to his sister a similar practice with regard to her own very different works. It is also possible that he credited her with the Horatian maxim that work should not appear till the ninth year. But while re-perusal in the ninth year may satisfy a poet that his lines have reached their final state, creative prose is, as Katherine Mansfield has written, 'never finished'.

The one certain indication of revision in this book is the men-tion of Scott with Cowper as a popular poet, which would not have been possible in 1798.[6] Miss Lascelles makes the attractive suggestion that, in her last recension, Jane Austen made a creative use of *Marmion* (1808), deliberately allowing Edward Ferrars, in his prosaic account of his pleasure in the Devonshire landscape,[7] to echo mockingly the Scotch drover (in the Introduction to Canto Third), who scorns such comfortable scenes.

The echo is less exact than one could wish, but we may cer-tainly follow Miss Lascelles in her argument that Marianne's ex-treme sensibility to Cowper ('those beautiful lines which have frequently almost driven me wild'[8]) would be unlikely before the appearance of William Hayley's biography in 1803, with its publication of *The Castaway* and its poignant revelations about the poet's state of mind. It may well have been *The Castaway* that Edward Ferrars read without animation.

An insertion of this sort (even if we do not admit the intention of parodying *Marmion*) suggests that a creative rehandling of the MS was in progress, and not a mere revision. To those who ask why Jane Austen chose this book to rehandle, and left on one side *Pride and Prejudice*, a conjectural (but probable) answer may be given: she chose her first work. There is no reason to suppose that the epistolary *First Impressions* was at all superior to the narrative form (1798) of *Sense and Sensibility*, and every reason to suppose it very much inferior to the *Sense and Sensibility* of 1811. The *Pride and Prejudice* published in 1813 is, beyond question, a great ad-vance; it was in writing *Sense and Sensibility* that Jane Austen learned to make so great a step forward, and (in all probability) it is during the early years at Chawton that she underwent her greatest development as an author.

The use of the 1811–12 calendar for the time scheme of *Pride and Prejudice* indicates the time of its recension,[9] and that of the 1808–9 calendar for *Mansfield Park* suggests that a version of that novel was composed at that date;[10] unfortunately no such exact chronology can be made out for *Sense and Sensibility*, in which no precise date is mentioned. The final revision may well have taken place in 1809–10, the year before publication, and the first year at Chawton; unfortunately no letters survive to tell the story. On 25 April 1811, staying with Henry in London, she writes to Cassandra that she is occupied with the proofs.[11]

§2. The epistolary framework

It has always puzzled critics to say between whom the letters can have been exchanged in the epistolary *Elinor and Marianne*; in the present story, the sisters are never a night apart until Elinor's marriage. Nevertheless, even in the existing text, eight letters are quoted in part or in full: Willoughby's infamous letter to Marianne (183) returns her three notes (186–7); Lucy writes to Elinor (277–8) and to Edward (365); and Mrs Jennings (370–1) and John Dashwood (371) write to Elinor.

In addition to this we hear of letters from Sir John Middleton to Mrs Dashwood (23), from Mrs Dashwood to Sir John (24), from Eliza Williams to Colonel Brandon (63), Edward Ferrars to Lucy Steele (134), Elinor to Mrs Dashwood (160, 172, 203), Lady Middleton to Mrs Jennings (170), Mrs Dashwood to Marianne (202), Mrs John Dashwood to Lucy Steele (253–4), and correspondences in consequence of Marianne's illness between Elinor and Mrs Dashwood (310) and John Dashwood (371).

Further conjectures may be made. It is possible that in the first draft the sisters were sometimes separated: Elinor might have remained behind at Norland for a time at the beginning of the book, and Marianne might have gone alone to London with Mrs Jennings. It is difficult, however, to see how the story could have been told (if it were still substantially the same) without the clumsiness of confidantes; moreover, Lucy's story being a secret, there would be no one but herself to whom Elinor could write about it.

Some of Marianne's ecstasies may well have been parts of

15

letters to a sympathizing friend. And events now related in Colonel Brandon's story of Eliza, in Nancy Steele's account of the crisis in Harley Street, and in Willoughby's confession would not have required much transposition from epistolary form.

§3. Sensibility

In its first conception, the 'sensibility' of Marianne was undoubtedly a 'literary joke',[12] comparable with the romanticism of Catherine Morland in *Northanger Abbey*, and having its ascendance in the author's youthful parodies such as *Love and Freindship*. And although more serious meanings were to overlay this original conception, we are not to forget it. The literary joke remains for the fun of the thing, and because, in sober sadness, many of Marianne's aberrations are to be attributed to her aesthetic notions.

She lays an undue stress on the feelings, in herself or in others; Cowper has 'frequently almost driven' her 'wild', and 'rapturous delight' in drawing 'in her opinion could alone be called taste'.[13]

Because the objects of her enthusiasm are nobler than bonnets, young men and the novels of Mrs Radcliffe, we are apt to forget that her manner of speaking is nearly as exaggerated as Isabella Thorpe's gush; to the latter the 'simplicity and truth' of Eleanor Tilney is a corrective,[14] as the former is corrected by the simplicity and truth of Elinor Dashwood.

Marianne may be called sincere, with the restriction that must be made when that word is applied to people so deficient in self-knowledge; she had no doubt persuaded herself that she felt about poetry as she would like to feel (and she did not much care for that of Pope, which demands a different sort of appreciation);[15] she certainly felt Willoughby's departure from Barton too much for tolerable composure: 'the feelings which made such a composure a disgrace, left her in no danger of incurring it'.[16]

She was much in need of the advice given to Captain Benwick by Anne Elliot, who 'thought it was the misfortune of poetry, to be seldom safely enjoyed by those who enjoyed it completely; and that the strong feelings which alone could estimate it truly, were the very feelings which ought to taste it but sparingly'.[17] She could have done very well with a 'larger allowance of prose'[18] in her daily study, particularly of works 'calculated to rouse and fortify the mind by the highest precepts'. For want of such a corrective—

of any sound moral instruction—she easily fell into the romantic error of 'the holiness of the heart's affections', believing second attachments to be impossible, and first attachments to have a force and an authority which neither could be gainsaid, nor should be if they could.

Like Colonel Brandon, we may see something 'amiable in the prejudices of a young mind',[19] and Marianne, even at the beginning of the book, is intended to be a charming girl and to make a deep appeal to the reader's sympathy. Nevertheless, Elinor is hardly too elder-sisterly when she sees 'inconveniences' attending such feelings as Marianne's.[20] She, herself, twice comes in for petulant misconception from her sister: "But I see what you mean. I have been too much at my ease, too happy, too frank. I have erred against every commonplace notion of decorum. . . . Had I talked only of the weather and the roads, and had I spoken only once in ten minutes, this reproach would have been spared."[21] And: "I thought it was right . . . to be guided wholly by the opinion of other people. I thought our judgments were given us merely to be subservient to those of our neighbours. This has always been your doctrine, I am sure."[22]

When she hears of Elinor's heroic self-command, Marianne's first thought is that her sister's feelings could never have been strong: "If such is your way of thinking . . . if the loss of what is most valued is so easily to be made up by something else, your resolution, your self-command, are, perhaps, a little less to be wondered at."[23] Even after she is greatly perfected, she will hardly be equal to heroism such as that of Elinor, when Edward calls at Barton after his supposed marriage with Lucy: 'with a countenance meaning to be open, she sat down again and talked of the weather'.[24] But by then Marianne had greatly suffered from the 'inconveniences' attending her feelings, and had learned in a hard school that much in her original system was dangerously silly, and that some of it was really wicked.

§4. Passion

Such a system as Marianne's predisposes to love. At the age of sixteen and a half, she did not believe that a worthy object would ever come her way.[25] *Nondum amabat, sed amare amabat*; anyone who knew her could have foreseen that she would not long escape.

Willoughby appeared in his shooting-jacket, and was all that her fancy had delineated as the man who could satisfy her ideas of perfection.[26] In such a costume Valancourt first appeared to Emily in *The Mysteries of Udolpho*, and it is not unlike a game-keeper's outfit.

Marianne's pleasure in his gay and charming companionship is but too natural—and there is no need to depreciate his attractive-ness—Elinor really loves him.[27] If we call him a 'simulacrum' or a 'figment' of Marianne's imagination, as Miss Lascelles does,[28] it is no more justified than it would be of the vast majority of lovers in fact or fiction. He begins, not unnaturally, with a flirtation, with no other view than to pass his time pleasantly while obliged to remain in Devonshire;[29] but he is hardly more reprehensible than the worthy Edward, who found female companionship an alleviation of his unhappiness in Sussex. He, far more than Mari-anne, finds himself caught; he has really fallen in love, and intends to propose on the very day when he is forced to take his departure. This would have wrecked his career—for he needed to marry money—and by anyone but Elinor he may be forgiven for think-ing that Marianne had less to risk, only a broken heart, which seldom has effects so lasting as those of an imprudent marriage. It is not as if Willoughby's own heart were unscathed.

He is pursued by bad luck. He was so unfortunate as to get that poor, dreadful Miss Williams with child, and he was also unfortu-nate that she behaved in a way to throw the utmost discredit on him; and when he left Barton in October, he can have had no expectation of being pursued to London by Marianne. His vices find him out, and are punished in such an exemplary way that, were he a character in 'real life', we might think that Providence was especially interested in the salvation of his soul; as he is a character in fiction, we are bound to think that the author was interested in saving some degree of credit for him.

The opportunity of following Willoughby to London finally overthrows Marianne. Elinor saw 'to what indifference to almost everything else, she was carried by her eagerness to be with Willoughby again',[30] and was disturbed to realize Marianne's terrible singleness of purpose 'in her pursuit of one object'.[31] Marianne's spirits soared as the journey was planned, but in London 'there was a flutter in them',[32] and soon she was in a piti-able state of anxiety for Willoughby's appearance. The impatience of lovers at this stage can be amusing even to kindly spectators, and the reader, like Elinor, is 'diverted'[33] as well as pained by Marianne's weather forecasts, as she looks for signs of a frost that will spoil Willoughby's sport, and drive him up to London.

The crisis comes. Willoughby's language[34] is flat and base, as it had been[35] on the day of his departure from Barton, when 'a sense of guilt almost took from' him 'the power of dissembling'. Had he been 'deep in hardened villany',[36] he would have put on a better act on each of these occasions. The wound to Marianne is piercing, and we can seriously believe that it may be mortal.

Next day, 'a cold, gloomy morning in January, Marianne, only half dressed, was kneeling against one of the window-seats for the sake of the little light she could command from it, and writing as fast as a continual flow of tears would permit her'.[37] This dreadful scene of the composition of her last letter to Willoughby, is succeeded by the animal agony into which she is thrown by his heartless reply: she was 'almost choked by grief . . . unable to speak . . . almost screamed with agony'.[38]

George Moore has well written of the 'almost animal emotion that consumed Marianne when she went up to London in search of Willoughby'.[39] Few writers have had the courage to represent a heroine in the grip of a passion as physical as influenza. Indeed, compared with Marianne, it may well be asked what character in English prose fiction may be said to be convincingly in love: Pip, perhaps, in *Great Expectations*. Indeed, if you go outside prose or outside English literature, there would not be many additions to the list.

It is astonishing that Mr E. M. Forster could write that Jane Austen 'faces the facts, but they are not her facts, and her lapses of taste over carnality can be deplorable, no doubt because they arise from lack of feeling'.[40] Mr Forster was being rather 'missish' about the jest (in a private letter to her sister) about the still-born child of Mrs Hall of Sherborne; research has not yet shown us that she had any reason for 'feeling' about this item of news.

It is a very great mistake to make an ill-considered charge against Jane Austen; it may well come back at you like a boomerang. Mr Forster once wrote a *Sense and Sensibility* (*Howard's End*), in which he notoriously failed to face the facts of life. At the end of the book, Helen Schlegel has a natural child, and many readers have found it incredible; the story requires that, for a great part of it, she should be 'on heat', obsessed (as Dr C. S. Lewis would say)[41] by Venus rather than by Eros—and such facts were not her author's, and he has not faced them. *Amicus Forster, magis amica Jane Austen* or, as Mr Shandy might translate, 'Mr Forster is my aunt, but Jane Austen is my sister.'

Marianne, of course, could never have a natural child; there was no danger of such a thing. 'Who can tell', Colonel Brandon asks, 'what were his [Willoughby's] designs on her?'[42] And Marianne, back at Barton, tells Elinor of her horrible suspicions of Willoughby's designs,[43] and her shame at having exposed herself to anything of the sort. She would be content to believe him 'only fickle', and this his confession to Elinor entitles her to do. According to Willoughby's own account, his feelings towards Marianne developed from 'selfish vanity'[44] to honourable intentions; and so near Allenham, and his respected relation Mrs Smith, it is hardly likely that he would have purposed seduction.

The poor, dreadful Miss Williams was exposed to Willoughby by 'the violence of her passions, the weakness of her understanding';[45] 'ranging over the town'[46] of Bath as she chose, with a silly school-friend, she had no protection. Marianne was in the bosom of her family, and though her affection for Willoughby was 'hardly less warm' than that of Eliza Williams, her mind was 'Oh! how infinitely superior!'[47]

In any case, she was as safe as if 'legions of liveried angels lackeyed her'. Jane Austen could not let a heroine fall from virtue. There are two reasons for this. The first is good taste: she wishes to spare the reader a shock that would be unaesthetic. Good manners must be the second reason: she will not ask the reader to meet a fallen woman. Lydia Bennet's offence is sufficiently covered up by marriage, and she herself a sufficiently trivial person, for her visit to Longbourn to be tolerated. But Maria is not received at Mansfield Park after her divorce, for Sir Thomas Bertram would not offer 'so great an insult to the neighbourhood'[48] as to expect it to notice her, even if there were no young person of either sex 'to be endangered by the society or hurt by the character of Mrs Rushworth'. Jane Austen will not hurt or endanger any young person, nor will she insult any older reader by expecting him to notice an adulteress. She may be right. The prohibition to cast the first stone at an adulteress does not mean that we are to admire her, and it applies only to life—in fiction an adulteress has sometimes been put there on purpose to be stoned, and if we stone her we are often stoning our own hearts, which may be the better for it.

Characters in fiction not having immortal souls, we have no duties towards them (such as charity and the like). We have, however, duties to ourselves in regard to them; we must not take hurt from their society, from adopting their conduct or their point of view. If Lady Chatterley were not such a bore, one might be tempted to think her a potential danger to young persons.

§5. Candour

'Like half the rest of the world, if more than half there be that are clever and good, Marianne, with excellent abilities and an excellent disposition, was neither reasonable nor candid. She expected from other people the same opinions and feelings as her own, and she judged of their motives by the immediate effect of their actions on herself.'[49] And Marianne's lack of 'candour' (the desire to make the best of other people) has resulted in 'an un-candid attitude to society and a refusal to take her part as a member of society'.[50]

This lack of candour is partly to be attributed to her romantic 'sensibility'. Soulful young people in every age have been 'un-candidly' contemptuous of those who did not share their enthusiasms; we have all been through this stage, and can only hope that there was something amiable in the prejudices of our young minds. Marianne had the disadvantage of having a mother not much wiser than herself, and of being so attractive as to disarm mockery.

Elinor, only two years older, has tried in vain to bring Marianne to treat their acquaintance in general with 'greater attention'.[51] She 'had never much toleration for any thing like impertinence, vulgarity, inferiority of parts, or even difference of taste from herself'.[52] She may be excused for her coldness to the Steeles, but hardly for her 'inattention to the forms of general civility'.[53] When she walks uninvited, and with a few brusque words, to the pianoforte at Barton Park, Lady Middleton is justified in feeling thankful that '*she* had never made so rude a speech'; and there is pleasant irony in Lucy and Elinor talking secrets while she was 'giving them the powerful protection of a very magnificent concerto'.

But Marianne's superiority and selfishness are naturally very much increased when passion aggravates 'sensibility': among the daughters of *Luxuria* (and Marianne's passion can surely be called 'lust', in all the dreadful meaning of Shakespeare's sonnet 129), St Thomas Aquinas enumerates 'caecitas mentis, inconsideratio, praecipitatio, amor sui'.[54] In blindness of mind, inconsideration, precipitation and egoism, she accepts an invitation to stay with Mrs Jennings, whose manners had ever been wounding to her 'irritable feelings',[55] and repays her kindness with nothing but 'ungrateful contempt'.[56]

Mrs Leavis[57] finds in Marianne's lack of candour, and her subsequent reformation, the central and most serious subject of the book. This is, perhaps, to go too far. Candour was certainly a subject of the greatest interest to Jane Austen, and a theme on which she was undoubtedly preaching to herself—Elizabeth Bennet's 'Prejudice' is, precisely, want of 'candour'. And Mrs Leavis well reminds us of the Austen family's tendency to 'clannish self-sufficiency'[58] (like that of Mr John Knightley) and Jane Austen's own efforts to combat it. A large, united and intelligent family must always be tempted to look down on outsiders, and a woman of Jane Austen's extraordinary gifts, living in a narrow neighbourhood, must have almost overwhelming temptations towards an uncandid attitude to society. She would not have regarded the theme as trivial, nor should we: Marianne has, as a besetting sin, a lack of justice, and she habitually neglects a large part of her duty to her neighbour.

Nevertheless, it is much to bring Marianne to the brink of the grave to teach her good manners, and I think the emphasis should be slightly shifted. Her lack of candour, and her uncandid attitude to society derive from uncorrected sensibility. What, no doubt, began as a literary joke, has acquired the utmost seriousness. Romanticism makes Catherine Morland behave in a way that is silly, and Marianne in a way that is selfish and sometimes unkind. This bad behaviour, however, is only symptomatic of a wrong view of life, which can lead to such appalling results as death, dishonour or mental derangement. *Sense and Sensibilty* is not a simple cautionary tale: 'Marianne Dashwood neglected the practice of general civility, and was punished by disappointment in love and a putrid fever.' It is, on the contrary, one of the most serious novels in the language, and teaches an important moral lesson with unrivalled eloquence. We may, in a way, regret that the author came so early to the handling of what, perhaps, was her greatest theme—there are clumsinesses and imperfections—but the violence of the passion that is central to the story could not be bettered.

*

Marianne's confession to Elinor is generous, and like herself. It falls into three parts, of which the first and last are by far the most serious. 'I saw that my own feelings had prepared my sufferings, and that my want of fortitude under them had almost led me to the grave. My illness, I well knew, had been entirely brought on by myself, by such negligence of my own health, as I had felt even at the time to be wrong. Had I died—it would have been self-destruction. . . . I wonder at my recovery,—wonder that the very eagerness of my desire to live, to have time for atonement to my God, and to you all, did not kill me at once.'[59] This is the language of 'seriousness', whether in Jane Austen's own time or in any other; Marianne is making an act of contrition for her sins against God— '*my* God', she says. *Deus, deus meus.*

The second part concerns her sins against her neighbours: 'Whenever I looked towards the past, I saw some duty neglected, or some failing indulged. Every body seemed injured by me. The kindness, the unceasing kindness of Mrs Jennings, I had repaid with ungrateful contempt. To the Middletons, the Palmers, the Steeles, to every common acquaintance even, I had been insolent and unjust. . . . To John, to Fanny,—yes, even to them, little as they deserve, I had given less than their due.'[60] The third part is a moving acknowledgement of her selfishness towards Elinor, and it includes self-reproach for leaving her alone in the discharge of 'offices of general complaisance or particular gratitude'.

The reader is certainly inclined to think that Marianne has nothing to reproach herself for as far as John and Fanny are concerned. Mrs Leavis makes this interesting comment: 'this strikes the reader as excessive and betrays that the author is trying to convince herself as well as us that *any* instinctive dislike of people as individuals should be smothered in an obligation to fit in with society'.[61] I think, however, that it is not Jane Austen who is speaking; it is Marianne, and she is speaking in character—she still exaggerates. We need not accuse her of lack of complaisance to John and Fanny; we should not have accused her of self-destruction had she died at Cleveland.

23

§6. Sense

Elinor is often found uninteresting by readers, and is regarded as a mere foil to Marianne; it is true that she is less completely created than she must have been had she been a heroine in a later novel. Too much of her is given in summary, in proportion to the scenes where she is allowed to reveal herself. Too many of her speeches are bookish, and might as well have been reported. She retains much of what, in *Elinor and Marianne*, must have been her original character, as a lay-figure of anti-Romanticism. But it is impossible to believe that by 1811 Jane Austen did not wish every principal character to have some degree of life and idiosyncracy, and it is possible to make a modest claim to these qualities for Elinor Dashwood.

The story reveals her coolness of judgement, her unselfishness in all the common offices of civility, and her quiet stoicism in her disappointed love: a composure of mind 'the effect of constant and painful exertion',[62] the opposite of Marianne's selfish abandonment to sorrow.

A wry humour endears her to the reader, and at times is a small consolation to herself.

' "And how does dear, dear Norland look?" cried Marianne.

' "Dear, dear Norland," said Elinor, "probably looks much as it always does at this time of the year. The woods and walks thickly covered with dead leaves."

' "Oh!" cried Marianne, "with what transporting sensations have I formerly seen them fall! How have I delighted, as I walked, to see them driven in showers about me by the wind! What feelings have they, the season, the air altogether inspired! Now there is no one to regard them. They are seen only as a nuisance, swept hastily off, and driven as much as possible from the sight."

' "It is not every one," said Elinor, "who has your passion for dead leaves." '[63]

Her quiet answers to the Steeles are admirable.

' "I confess . . . that while I am at Barton Park, I never think of tame and quiet children with any abhorrence." '[64]

And when Nancy Steele pretends to be afraid that her cousins will tease her about her 'beau', Dr Davies:

24

' "Well . . . it is a comfort to be prepared against the worst. You have got your answer ready." '[65]

Her greatest triumphs, when her wry humour is directed against herself, are not spoken aloud.

Mrs Jennings brings for Marianne a glass of the old Constantia, that so benefited her late husband whenever he had a touch of his old cholicky gout. Elinor drinks it herself, reflecting that 'though its good effects on a cholicky gout were, at present, of little importance to her, its healing powers on a disappointed heart might be as reasonably tried on herself as on her sister'.[66]

More than Marianne, Elinor, for all her good manners, deserved that Lady Middleton should fancy her 'satirical';[67] and, like her creator, she was comforted by the possession of a satirical wit in a Cinderella life, among the Ferrars and Dashwoods. A more poignant experience that she must have shared with Jane Austen is the following: 'Without shutting herself up from her family, or leaving the house in determined solitude to avoid them, or lying awake the whole night in meditation, Elinor found every day afforded her leisure enough to think. . . . There were moments in abundance, when, if not by the absence of her mother and sisters, at least by the nature of their employments, conversation was forbidden among them, and every effect of solitude was produced. Her mind was inevitably at liberty; her thoughts could not be chained elsewhere.'[68]

§7. Money

Several critics have observed that in each of Jane Austen's novels there is a Cinderella situation. In *Sense and Sensibility* Elinor and Marianne are turned out of the family place by their father's untimely death; and their great-uncle's injudicious will leaves them, their mother and Margaret with a very modest income.

Marianne is too romantic to think about money (beyond fixing on £2,000 a year as a competence).[69] It is Elinor who is the Cinderella, always made conscious of the Ferrars family's disapproval of her as a possible wife for Edward, because she could only bring him £1,000.

Edward was 'the eldest son of a man who had died very rich', and we may suspect that at one time at least Jane Austen had thought of the Ferrars family—for all the romantic associations of the name—as connected with trade. Edward's mother and sister wish to see him distinguished 'as—they hardly knew what'. It does not look as if there were any tradition in the family for him to follow. His uncle, Sir Robert[70] (from his influence with her, he was probably Mrs Ferrars' brother—and it is to the second son that he gives his name) was very likely a carpet knight, and of no more distinction than Sir William Lucas.

It is one of the happy ironies of the plot that it is Elinor who makes the marriage of 'sensibility'; she marries her first love, and if they do not settle down to love in a cottage ('they were neither of them quite enough in love to think that three hundred and fifty pounds a-year would supply them with the comforts of life'),[71] eight hundred and fifty was as much 'as was desired, and more than was expected'[72]—for Elinor had regarded one thousand as wealth.[73] It is precisely people like Elinor (and Mrs Jennings, who shares her 'bourgeois' view of money: "the Colonel is a ninny, my dear; because he has two thousand a-year himself, he thinks that nobody else can marry on less")[74]—people who concede that a little money is necessary for the external comforts of life—who know how little is really necessary.

To be as indifferent to money as Marianne, you need to have a lot of it, or to be possessed of a Skimpole talent for living on other people. You expect: 'A proper establishment of servants, a carriage, perhaps two, and hunters',[75] not to speak of 'loose cash' for improving your 'collection of music and books'.[76] Not for you a snug cottage with 'two maids and two men',[77] still less a poor curate's misery, with only 'a stout girl of all works'[78] (Edward and Elinor were not enough in love for that).

Marianne has fallen in love with an expensive young man, whose property at Combe Magna was not equal to his wishes; even before his majority, he had begun to get into debt, and though he is likely to inherit a good property at Allenham, 'that event being uncertain, and possibly far distant',[79] he is obliged to plan a mercenary marriage. Elinor is obviously right in thinking that a marriage between Willoughby and Marianne 'on a small, very small income'[80] (they would only have had £750 a year between them) would have made Willoughby very unhappy. It may also be questioned whether, as a poor man, Willoughby would have been so interesting to her; much of his charm depended on 'dashing about with his curricle and hunters';[81] Edward, who had no sporting and dramatic appearance to keep up, would wear far better in comparative poverty; he had, indeed, no talent for being expensive.

However, at nineteen, and 'with no sentiment superior to strong esteem and lively friendship', [82] Marianne married Colonel Brandon—who was possessed of the necessary two thousand a year—only two years after her first meeting with Willoughby. Some readers have thought it a little soon; later, Jane Austen was careful not to set a date to the transference of Edmund's affections to Fanny, being 'aware that the cure of unconquerable passions, and the transfer of unchanging attachments, must vary much as to time in different people'. [83]

§8. Irony

This is less of a 'detective story' than *Pride and Prejudice* or *Emma*, and there are few clues to the only mystery: Edward's secret engagement to Lucy.

On hearing of the Dashwoods' projected move to Barton, Edward 'in a voice of surprise and concern, which required no explanation to' Mrs Dashwood, repeated: "Devonshire! Are you, indeed, going there? So far from hence; And to what part of it?" [84] When he came to Barton 'he had been in Devonshire a fortnight . . . He looked rather distressed as he added, that he had been staying with some friends near Plymouth.' [85]

When the Steeles come to Barton, Nancy, vulgar and familiar as she is, yet surprises Elinor by a question about Norland. Lucy adds, by way of apology, "We have heard Sir John admire it excessively." [86] An attentive reader may remember that there is a strong indication that he was never there: 'He had formerly visited at Stanhill, but it was too long ago for his young cousins to remember him.' [87]

Both in the pattern of the plot and its conclusion Jane Austen shows the ironical power that will be so superbly exercised in scenes in the later novels. The finest example is the great chapter in which Elinor helps Lucy Steele with her filigree basket.

Elinor reopens the interesting subject of the secret engagement, and Lucy warmly thanks her; she had been afraid of having given offence.

' "Offended me! How could you suppose so? Believe me," and Elinor spoke with the truest sincerity, "nothing could be farther from my intention, than to give you such an idea." ' This is masterly, and the next words are barbed ' "Could you have a motive for the trust, that was not honourable and flattering to me?" ' She knows that Lucy's motive was to give pain, and to warn her off the ground.

Lucy, 'her little sharp eyes full of meaning,' replies (rubbing salt into the wound): "There seemed to me to be a coldness and displeasure in your manner, that made me quite uncomfortable." No wonder, for, well as she had concealed it, Elinor had been 'mortified, shocked, confounded'.

After further fencing between the rivals, Lucy mentions Robert Ferrars as 'a great coxcomb', which brings in this chorus from the card-table:

' "A great coxcomb!" repeated Miss Steele, whose ear had caught those words by a sudden pause in Marianne's music.—"Oh! they are talking of their favourite beaux, I dare say."

' "No, sister," cried Lucy, "you are mistaken there, our favourite beaux are *not* great coxcombs."

' "I can answer for it that Miss Dashwood's is not," said Mrs Jennings, laughing heartily; "for he is one of the modestest, prettiest behaved young men I ever saw; but as for Lucy, she is such a sly little creature, there is no finding out who *she* likes."

' "Oh!" cried Miss Steele, looking significantly round at them, "I dare say Lucy's beau is quite as modest and pretty behaved as Miss Dashwood's" '—for she knows that he is the same person.[88]

§9. The Anti-heroines

I. THE STEELES

Nancy Steele is silliness incarnate, and Lucy lack of sensibility: in their first conception they may have been something like dummies, in the moral pageant of Elinor and Marianne. But Jane Austen had in life enough models for impertinence and vulgarity to give them a dreadful idiosyncrasy of their own. Their bad grammar is unforgettable and (as their uncle has a tutorial establishment) unforgivable. Both are toadies, and affect to be sentimental baby-worshippers, in contradistinction to the 'satirical' Dashwoods; they are therefore desirable guests for the vapid Lady Middleton, and they expose her claim to elegance—no really refined woman could have endured their company. Lucy, younger and much shrewder, has some perceptions, at least, of her sister's inferiority in sense and manners, and can adapt herself with success to the world of Mrs Ferrars and the John Dashwoods (which seems to have a degree more of refinement than that of Barton Park). Elinor has said that she 'does not want sense, and that is the foundation on which every good thing may be built', and has declared her, not only in person but also in understanding, 'superior to half her sex'.[89] But she is a gold-digger, and that is the use she makes of her sense (so completely severed from sensibility). Her engagement to Edward may have been formed before she was old enough for calculation, and she has wit enough to make him continue to think her 'a well-disposed, good-hearted girl, and thoroughly attached to himself'[90]—otherwise he would, and easily could, have released himself from an entanglement dating from his minority: Mrs Ferrars might have been ill-tempered about it, but she would have paid off Lucy. He felt himself tied to her not (as some, including myself at one time, have thought) by a mistaken sense of honour, but by emotional responsibility. When the crisis came, Edward believed that nothing 'but the most disinterested affection was her inducement' to choose to continue the engagement. Nancy repeated the affecting conversation to Elinor: "She had not the least mind in the world to be off, for she could live with him upon a trifle, and how little so ever he might have, she should be very glad to have it all, you know, or something of the kind."[91] Jane Austen is here reverting from fiction to pure burlesque but, nevertheless, it is not far from the truth of the situation. Elinor's summing-up commands assent: "She lost nothing by continuing the engagement, for she has proved that it fettered neither her inclinations nor her actions. The connection was certainly a respectable one, . . . and if nothing more advantageous occurred it would be better for her to marry *you* than be single."[92] If Robert Ferrars had not appeared—thrown, as it seems, by the author to Lucy in a desperate attempt to save her heroine's lover —Edward must have been lost.

2. THE JENNINGS FAMILY

Mrs Jennings, and her daughters, Lady Middleton and Charlotte Palmer, are also 'up to a point, parodies of the two heroines and their mother', as a recent critic[93] has observed. Mrs Jennings, solidly sensible about money, where Mrs Dashwood is foolish, can sometimes make even practical common sense absurd: "Oh! 'tis a nice place! A butcher hard by in the village, and the parsonage-house within a stone's throw. To my fancy, a thousand times prettier than Barton Park, where they are forced to send three miles for their meat, and have not a neighbour nearer than your mother."[94]

I cannot, however, follow Mr Gillie entirely in thinking that Lady Middleton's anxiety for decorum and her over-indulgence of her children mark her as a 'devotee of sensibility', or that Charlotte Palmer's facile good nature is 'a kind of sense'. Charlotte surely stands for silliness. Like Mr Bennet, Mr Palmer, 'captivated by youth and beauty, and that appearance of good humour, which youth and beauty generally give',[95] had married a woman lacking in sense (Charlotte was very pretty, and Mr Gillie can hardly be right in suggesting that she was married for her money). Lady Middleton's cold insipidity is as surely the opposite of sensibility; and as sensibility has its 'inconveniences', it is fitting that on occasion she should have very much better manners than Marianne. Nevertheless, apart from her affection for her children (which is essentially self-indulgent) she has no warmth of heart, and is a fit associate for Fanny Dashwood and Sophia Willoughby.

Though 'up to a point' the Jennings sisters are parodies of Elinor and Marianne, Mrs Leavis is nearer to the truth in saying that 'they have the function of providing contrasts favourable to their mother', though she goes far in saying that they 'are not meant to be plausible persons'.[96] It is difficult to believe that by 1811 Jane Austen did not mean all her persons to be, in the main, plausible; though, in the palimpsests that her novels are, a word or phrase of pure burlesque will remain, either because she let it slip through or (probably more often) because she could not bring herself to sacrifice it to plausibility. But while persons in themselves are meant to be plausible, she has not troubled so much about the plausibility of the relations between them—Dr Chapman[97] has observed how little she cares about establishing family resemblances, and she will postulate (without any explanation) friendship between very ill-matched people (for example, John Thorpe and James Morland).

Lady Middleton, indeed, is barely characterized—unless it is more true to say that her character is to have no character at all. Mrs Palmer, however, talks with a genuine and often engaging vivacity, and laughs with a maddening laugh that may well be drawn from life.

Against the vapid conventionality of Lady Middleton, and the silliness of Mrs Palmer, the warm-hearted, vulgar, sensible Mrs Jennings stands out in her full value and (as Mrs Leavis rightly points out) it is she who pronounces the final judgement on the baseness of some of the other characters, and we accept her verdict. Apart from Colonel Brandon—and that worthy man is a 'stick' if ever there was one—she is the only sensible adult person in the book. I do not think those critics are right who see either a change or development in her character, or a change in the author's attitude to her. We see her through Elinor's eyes, and Elinor discovers her sterling worth upon further acquaintance with her. It is Marianne's unhappiness which gives her the opportunity to exercise virtues of a sort to make her vulgarity and bad taste matters of no importance in comparison.

§10. The Plot

The main plot, the sentimental education of Marianne, is also an ironical commentary on sensibility. 'She was born to discover the falsehood of her own opinions, and to counteract, by her conduct, her most favourite maxims.' A prudent marriage, after she has 'overcome an affection formed so late in life as seventeen', makes her 'the mistress of a family, and the patroness of a village',[98] where Elinor has settled down with her first love, and on less than half the income of the Brandons.

Marianne's lover, Willoughby, the only person in the book who has to suffer a moral conflict, chooses money instead of love, and regrets his choice. Elinor is hard on him in pointing out how much he would have regretted the alternative choice—if he had chosen love, money would (in the end) have been added to him. He was reinstated as heir to Allenham by Mrs Smith who, 'by stating his marriage with a woman of character, as the source of her clemency, gave him reason for believing that had he behaved with honour towards Marianne, he might at once have been happy and rich'[99] —Elinor, however, could not at the time know this. Some sort of happiness is promised him, though he has missed a higher happiness; and he will always be a nicer person for his experience. The author who, like Elinor, loved him, has, in a way, saved him.

Edward, in this formal comedy, has a role that balances that of Willoughby; he is torn between love and (what he conceives to be) duty. He never even admits to himself that there can be a legitimate choice, and he is rewarded for faithfulness to duty by love, and a modest competence. His role is a dull one and, as his appeal is to sense rather than to sensibility, he is forced to appear unattractive. Marianne, on occasion, can bring out a charming sly humour that he possesses—between them there is an affectionate brother and sister relationship of a kind that Jane Austen likes to have in every book, and that can only make this appearance in *Sense and Sensibility* (Edward's sister Fanny, and Marianne's half-brother John being incapable of such a thing).

Small clumsinesses in the plot would, probably, have been done away with if this work had come later in the canon. Something is done to cover them up, as if the author were painfully conscious of them. 'I come now,' she says, exceptionally speaking in the first person, 'to a misfortune, which about this time befell Mrs John Dashwood'[100]—this is to prepare the way for the very improbable invitation to the Misses Steele to stay with her in Harley Street. They have to go there, for the sake of the dénouement.

A much worse clumsiness, for it makes Elinor and still more her mother behave with an inconceivable lack of tenderness and imagination, is their obliging Marianne to remain on in London after her disappointment. It is necessary to the story that Elinor should remain in London, as witness to the development of the relations between Edward and Lucy, and it is unthinkable that she would have remained alone. But the arguments adduced by their mother in favour of a longer stay can deceive no one: 'A variety of occupations, of objects, and of company . . . might yet, she hoped, cheat Marianne, at times, into some interest beyond herself, and even into some amusement, much as the idea of both might now be spurned by her.'[101] Marianne might be forgiven if she felt desperate at her mother's offering such consolation—Mrs Jennings was more excusable for offering dried cherries, and the company of the Sandersons and the Parrys, for she knew no better.

Margaret, a character who only walks on, and who is forgotten by Marianne in her enumerations of those dear to her, ought, one feels, to justify her place in the book, or to be excluded from it.

She probably had no place in the epistolary *Elinor and Marianne*: if they were often separated (for the sake of a correspondence) one of them would always be with their mother. Margaret has been invented to be a companion to Mrs Dashwood—otherwise the only function she performs (and one by no means necessary) is to make Mrs Jennings and Sir John Middleton aware of an attachment between Edward and Elinor, a thing which they could easily have thought of for themselves.

Pride and Prejudice

§1. Its History

In Cassandra Austen's note, we are told that *First Impressions* was written between October 1796 and August 1797; that is, after the writing of *Elinor and Marianne* in epistolary form, and before its first recension as *Sense and Sensibility*. In the November following its completion, George Austen was offering it for publication to Cadell, a London publisher, in a rather unbusinesslike letter, from which it is not clear if it were to come out at the author's risk; Cadell declined to interest himself in it.[1]

In what form was *First Impressions* in 1797? Miss Lascelles[2] assumes that it was a 'piece of direct narrative writing' which showed the author what was her true form, and led to the recasting of *Elinor and Marianne*. Mrs Leavis[3] (with much more probability) assumes that it was in letter-form. There are two arguments in her favour; Mr Austen, in his letter, says it was 'about the length of Miss Burney's *Evelina*', and (as I hope to show) signs of an original epistolary form can be clearly discerned.

The manuscript continued to be read among Jane Austen's intimates. In January 1799 she writes to Cassandra (then at Godmersham): 'I do not wonder at your wanting to read "First Impressions" again, so seldom as you have gone through it, and that so long ago.'[4] And in June of the same year she writes from Bath (to her sister at Steventon): 'I would not let Martha [Lloyd] read "First Impressions" again upon any account, and am very glad that I did not leave it in your power. She is very cunning, but I saw through her design; she means to publish it from memory, and one more perusal must enable her to do it.'[5]

The next positive evidence is that of the *Life*[6]: 'by April 1811 *Sense and Sensibility* was in the printers' hands, and *Pride and Prejudice* far advanced'. Jane Austen, therefore, had started on this task before the success of her first publication came to encourage her. Dr Chapman shows that in this revision she almost certainly used the almanac for 1811 and 1812 for her time-scheme, and this suggests that a very considerable amount of re-writing was done at that time.

Unfortunately, there is a gap in the Letters from 6 June 1811 to 24 January 1813, bridged only by a letter to Martha Lloyd of 29 November 1812, in which she says that 'P. & P. is sold.'[7] Publication took place in January 1813, and the author received her copy. She wrote to her sister: 'I have lop't and crop't so successfully, however, that I imagine it must be rather shorter than S. & S.'[8] This only justifies us in saying that some excision had been done, but later she says: 'I am exceedingly pleased that you can say what you do, having gone thro' the whole work.'[9] Cassandra had 'gone through' *First Impressions* often enough; perhaps she had not 'gone through' the altered *Pride and Prejudice*. So argues Miss Lascelles;[10] but I cannot, myself, derive any comfort from this argument. I am convinced that Cassandra 'went through' the book at every stage, and that this passage refers only to her first reading of it in print. As Jane Austen and her sister were writing about subjects very familiar to them both, we must expect *lacunae* in the evidence, from our point of view.

Finally, Dr Chapman raises another query; 'What it was that Miss Austen "Lop't and Crop't" we cannot know. It may have been *First Impressions*; it may equally have been a later version.'[11]

This book, therefore, contains work by the author from at least 1796 until 1812; we cannot tell how many recensions of it were made between those dates, and though criticism may hope sometimes to detect earlier or later strata in it, scholarship, unfortunately, has no real help to give.

§2. The epistolary framework

The epistolary framework of this novel is much more apparent than that of *Sense and Sensibility*. The two heroines, Jane and Elizabeth Bennet, are separated for about four and a half months out of the whole twelve-month (and a little more) during which the action takes place.

On 30 December 1811 Jane goes to London[12] to stay with the Gardiners. Early in the following March, Elizabeth sees her briefly when she passes through London, on the way to stay with Mr and Mrs Collins at Hunsford. They are not reunited till 18 April, when Elizabeth comes back from Kent. They are separated again from about 15 July to 8 August, when Elizabeth is travelling with the Gardiners.

In the course of the book, twenty-one letters are quoted or given in full, and a further twenty-two letters are mentioned or implied. Apart from occasional letters from one character to another, there are several regular correspondences: between Jane and Elizabeth, between both sisters and Mrs Gardiner, between Elizabeth and Charlotte Collins, between Jane and Caroline Bingley, and between the Collins and Lucas families. Several letters reveal facts of the first importance.

§3. *Sense and Sensibility* and *Pride and Prejudice*

The two novels have many similarities of pattern and theme. Each is the story of two mutually devoted sisters who, after various vicissitudes, both make happy marriages, by which they are not widely separated. If the two stories contain an element of wish-fulfilment, it is not surprising; but if such a feeling lay behind the original impulse, it has since been exposed to merciless self-criticism.

The two sisters, like Elinor and Marianne, represent 'candour' and 'prejudice'; but Elizabeth, the 'uncandid' sister, has a large proportion of Elinor's good sense. Marianne bore some physical resemblance to her author; she had 'the advantage of height'[13] over Elinor, and Jane Austen's stature 'could not have been increased without exceeding the middle height'.[14] Marianne was perhaps darker, 'but from its transparency, her complexion was uncommonly brilliant', while Henry Austen says of his sister (beautifully adapting Donne's *Second Anniversary*) that 'her eloquent blood spoke through her modest cheek'. In *Pride and Prejudice*, while it is reasonable to see much of the tender-hearted Cassandra in Jane Bennet, most readers have seen a great deal of Jane Austen's personality in Elizabeth—whose wit, after all, must be the author's own.

There is a further likeness in the basic pattern: the 'candid' sister (Elinor or Jane) is united to the man whom she loved from the beginning of the book. The 'uncandid' sister (Marianne or Elizabeth) is punished by being imposed on by an anti-hero (Willoughby or Wickham), but ends by making an advantageous marriage with a worthy man (Brandon or Darcy). In either case the anti-hero has antecedently injured the worthy man: Willoughby has seduced Colonel Brandon's ward, and Wickham has tried to elope with Georgiana Darcy. Their conduct is in either case rather clumsily revealed: to Elinor by Colonel Brandon, in a synopsis of previous events, and to Elizabeth by Darcy's letter. The revelation, in either case, provokes a revulsion of feeling, and is a turning-point; later Willoughby is finished off by a mercenary and Wickham by an immoral marriage.

Pride and Prejudice, in its latest recension, dates from after the latest recension of *Sense and Sensibility* on which, in most ways, it seems a great advance. This is all that the facts entitle us to say. We know that Jane Austen had been working on earlier drafts of each of them for more than fifteen years; when we find a similarity in theme or character between the two novels, we cannot say which was the earlier conception. We cannot even be sure that nothing has been transferred from one novel to the other.

Other parallels occur—themes, perhaps, which specially interested the writer (for one reason or another) and which she cared to explore more than once.

The married life of Mr Palmer, a sensible man with a pretty, silly wife, is studied, 'twenty years on', in that of Mr Bennet; the two vulgar Steele sisters, without very much change, become Kitty and Lydia; Aunt Philips, in her cosy, lower middle class good nature, is perhaps a rudimentary Mrs Jennings. Mr Collins, with his excessive deference for his patroness, Lady Catherine, has something of John Dashwood, and his submissive attitude to his wife and her mother. Here John Dashwood is the more interesting character—especially in his attempt to salve his own conscience by forming expectations that other people should provide for his half-sisters; and in Mr Collins (as often elsewhere) Jane Austen has isolated a single 'humour' for over-development.

§4. Burlesque and Imitation

The title is taken from the moral drawn in Fanny Burney's *Cecilia*: 'The whole of this unfortunate business . . . has been the result of PRIDE and PREJUDICE.'

Dr Chapman[15] points out other resemblances, and conjectures that *First Impressions* 'owed more to *Cecilia* than the alteration of its title'. Mrs Leavis[16] believes that it owed its existence.

On her theory it was an attempt to write, in realistic terms, the story of a girl who, like Cecilia, should be met with an appeal by an aristocratic lover's family to reject him, because she was not a suitable match. Cecilia yields to the appeal of Mrs Delvile; Elizabeth is confronted by Lady Catherine (the hero's aunt, not his mother—a further touch of the grotesque) and behaves as a rational young woman would. *First Impressions*, then, would have been a story like *Northanger Abbey*, also with an anti-heroine—one ' "pert" and of an on-coming disposition, just as necessarily as Catherine is green and dense'.

Mrs Leavis strengthens her case by showing that Mr Collins is a piece of pure parody of Fanny Burney: of her 'preposterous conventions about female behaviour', and of the ponderous, Johnsonian speech of her characters.

Overt and direct parody of Fanny Burney occurs at other places in the book. Mary's elegant extract,[17] from which she derives 'the balm of sisterly consolation' to pour into Elizabeth's wounded bosom, is from a letter of Mr Villars, the 'best of men', to Evelina: "Remember, my dear Evelina, nothing is so delicate as the reputation of a woman: it is, at once, the most beautiful and the most brittle of human things."[18]

Mr Bennet's termination of the scene following Mr Collins' proposal is brilliant, completely in character, and has all the air of a happy and spontaneous invention: "An unhappy alternative is before you, Elizabeth. From this day you must be a stranger to one of your parents.—Your mother will never see you again if you do *not* marry Mr Collins, and I will never see you again if you *do*."[19]

And yet this scene is even funnier if one thinks at the same time of that where Evelina has to reconcile loyalty to a dead mother (whom she never knew) with that to a new-found father (whom she sees for the first time). ' "Evelina," he cried, "she charges me to receive thee;—wilt thou in obedience to her will, own for thy father the destroyer of thy mother?" '[20] We know, from *Love and Freindship*, how very much Jane Austen had been amused at this scene.[21]

On the other hand, Fanny Burney is an 'influence' as well as a butt: the scene where Darcy's disparaging remark about Elizabeth is overheard at a ball, is adapted from that where Lord Orville speaks slightingly of Evelina on her first introduction into London life.

§5. Other sources

In 'Volume the Second' of Jane Austen's juvenilia, there is a most interesting document, a letter 'From a Young Lady in distressed Circumstances to her friend'. It is not burlesque, but a realistic account of the rudeness of a rich woman, Lady Grevile, to the poor and sensitive Maria Williams, and it looks remarkably like an experience witnessed or personally felt in 'real life'. Lady Grevile takes Maria to a ball, and the next day calls to ask her to dinner— obliging the girl to go out and stand by her coach-door in a cold wind.

Other critics have seen the similarity between Lady Grevile and Lady Catherine de Bourgh, and have compared the scene at the coach-door with Charlotte Collins' standing in the wind to talk to Miss de Bourgh in her carriage.

Mrs Leavis[23] convincingly shows that the letter contains also the germs of some of Miss Bingley's conversation, and of much of the character and conduct of Mrs Norris in *Mansfield Park*. She might (I think) have added that Lady Greville's second appearance (at the early and unfashionable dinner hour of humbler people) is a foretaste of the visit of Lord Osborne and Tom Musgrave to the Watsons.[24]

It cannot be doubted that Mrs Leavis is right in saying that Jane Austen's practice is 'rather thriftily to "make over" ' scenes and characters used before in her early burlesque writing, or observed in life. I am not, however, convinced that she deliberately used her volumes of juvenilia. She may, of course, actually have gone to them, as to a larder; she had carefully copied and preserved so many early pieces, and in a letter of 1814 she mentions the stage coach in *Love and Freindship*.[25] It seems to me more probable (though this we shall never know) that she cherished incidents, scenes and scraps of character in her mind, and there sorted and reworked them; the fact that some of them had found immature expression in her early writings would do much to fix them, and in this way the juvenilia are of the greatest interest to us, whether she ever looked at them again or not. In the same way, a writer may remember better an incident of which he has written in a letter, even if the letter is sent away and never seen again; but Jane

Austen, if she chose, could re-read all her old letters to Cassandra, and they might serve, like a diary, to revive old memories.

Hints from 'real life' must be treated with great caution, as we know Jane Austen's own care not to leave traces. We may, if we like, conjecture that her cousin, the Rev. Edward Cooper, with his ponderous sermons, and his 'letters of cruel comfort'[26] may have contributed a few touches to the character of Mr Collins, so long as we do not identify him with that character.

Indeed, Jane Austen's particular blend of burlesque and realism, her borrowing of themes both from literature and from life, and her patient working up of character and incident until she can use it in its final and most effective form, is precisely the method best adopted if she were to draw on an experience open to all her nearest connections, and yet give no offence to anyone by particular references. All her life and her reading went into her imagination, and thence, together, took a new concoction; indeed there is little that has been set before the reader until it has simmered for years and been boiled up afresh three or four times.

§6. 'Petulance and Acrimony'

There can be no doubt that, by the time of the publication of *Pride and Prejudice*, Jane Austen meant Darcy and Elizabeth to be plausible and attractive persons.

The very evening that the book arrived at Chawton (27 January 1813) Jane Austen and her mother read half the first volume aloud to Miss Benn: 'she really does seem to admire Elizabeth. I must confess that I think her as delightful a creature as ever appeared in print, and how I shall be able to tolerate those who do not like *her* at least I do not know.'[27] Fanny Knight's praise, about a fortnight later, was gratifying: 'Her liking Darcy and Elizabeth is enough, she might hate all the others if she would.'[28]

Readers and critics have been far from unanimous about Darcy, but few lovers of Jane Austen's novels have refused Elizabeth their wholehearted, if uncritical, admiration. And yet hers is a more complicated and interesting character than is generally perceived.

Traces of her original 'pertness' as an anti-Cecilia remain; there are at least two passages, no doubt dating from an early version, which, had we been in Cassandra's place, we should have recommended Jane Austen to strike out.

"There is a fine old saying, which every body here is of course familiar with—'Keep your breath to cool your porridge',—and I shall keep mine to swell my song."[29]

And: "Mr Darcy sends you all the love in the world, that he can spare from me."[30]

These embarrassingly tasteless remarks of Elizabeth are passed over, and this may be just as well, by those who read the book with uncritical admiration; they are also blind to more uncomfortable aspects of her personality, but this is a pity, for here some of the author's greatest skill has been shown. Elizabeth, like Catherine Morland and Marianne Dashwood before her, and like Emma Woodhouse later, is one of the heroines who have to go through a form of conversion (the seriousness of which varies from book to book); Dr C. S. Lewis[31] contrasts them with Fanny Price and Anne Elliot, 'the solitary heroines who make no mistakes'.

Mrs Leavis [32] rightly speaks of Jane Austen's preoccupation in this novel with marriage, and it is certain that, at least on some occasions during the fifteen years or so of the book's composition, the subject came very near to the author. In 1796 she no doubt took it for granted that she would marry some day—as her mother did, who, when welcoming Mary Lloyd into the family as her son James's second wife, anticipated comfort from her when Cassandra was gone into Shropshire (as the wife of Tom Fowle) and Jane 'the Lord knows where'.[33] It was, perhaps, as well for Mrs Austen that she did not have to rely upon the tender mercies of 'Mrs J. A.', who was not the most agreeable of women, and would probably come out in a worse light if more documents were left us. In 1812 Jane Austen probably took it for granted that marriage had passed her by.

In the meantime several events had occurred whose significance to her is not known to us. The letters tell us of a girlish flirtation with Tom Lefroy, and of the admiration of Samuel Blackall; family tradition (confused as to detail) records an attachment to a man, probably met in Devonshire in 1801 or 1802, who died before he had 'spoken';[34] in 1802 she declined the proposal of Harris Bigg-Wither of Manydown, a Hampshire neighbour six years younger than herself, whose sisters were her friends—it is related that she at first consented to marry him, but withdrew her acceptance on the following day;[35] it is not unlikely that she received a proposal from Edward Bridges, a younger brother of her sister-in-law, Elizabeth (another man younger than herself).[36]

It is probable that she had wished for marriage; it is certain (from the tone of her work, and from her refusal of the eligible Harris Bigg-Wither) that she would not have contemplated a marriage without affection. It is inconceivable that some of the women in her large family did not look down on her as an old maid, and let her know it.

Some of these preoccupations are undoubtedly expressed in the character of Elizabeth. Though always charming, witty and self-critical, and never selfish and unkind like Marianne Dashwood, Elizabeth is, for the greater part of the time, suffering from a frustration that is a constant temptation to 'petulance and acrimony'; sometimes it gets the better of her. Her frustration is not only sexual (from a failed love-affair, if it can be called so much), but also social and intellectual—it covers almost every aspect of her life except her affection for her sister Jane, and for that beloved sister's own sake she is compelled to have secrets from her.

The distress of Jane's disappointment, resulting from the flight of Bingley from Netherfield, the sickness of heart caused by Charlotte Lucas's mercenary marriage, provoke an expression of malaise too great for the occasion. 'The more I see of the world, the more I am dissatisfied with it; and every day confirms my belief of the inconsistency of all human characters and of the little dependence that can be placed on the appearance of either merit or sense. I have met with two instances lately; one I will not mention, the other is Charlotte's marriage. It is unaccountable! in every view it is unaccountable!'[37]

Jane is surely answering the tone more than the words, when she begins: "My dear Lizzy, do not give way to such feelings as these. They will ruin your happiness."

Elizabeth, at this time, was seeing a good deal of Wickham; we are not admitted into her own consciousness at this point, and merely observe her with the sharp but kindly eyes of Mrs Gardiner, who was made sufficiently uneasy by their apparent preference for each other to give her niece a caution.

The rhythm of Elizabeth's reply—good-humoured and honest though it is—reveals that she is not unaffected.

"At present I am not in love with Mr Wickham; no, I certainly am not. But he is, beyond all comparison, the most agreeable man I ever saw—and if he becomes really attached to me—I believe it will be better that he should not."[38]

She detached herself from him successfully, and 'without material pain'[39] saw his admiration transferred to Miss King, who had lately inherited ten thousand pounds. Nevertheless, in his farewell to her before her Kentish visit 'there was a solicitude, and interest which she felt must ever attach her to him with a most sincere regard; and she parted from him convinced, that whether married or single, he must always be her model of the amiable and pleasing'.[40]

On her way through London, she spoke to her aunt in a tone of complete disillusionment: ". . . I have a very poor opinion of young men who live in Derbyshire; and their intimate friends who live in Hertfordshire are not much better. I am sick of them all. Thank Heaven! I am going to-morrow where I shall find a man who has not one agreeable quality, who has neither manner nor sense to recommend him. Stupid men are the only ones worth knowing, after all."[41] Her aunt, who had been attempting to be 'candid', and would be sorry to think ill of Wickham, warns her that her speech 'savours strongly of disappointment'. It savours of more than disappointment; Elizabeth is going through a phase of sourness—it is more complicated and interesting than Marianne's ingrowing romanticism, and owes less to literature. We can see at once why Jane Austen postponed the development of this theme, until after she had tackled the simpler subject of *Sense and Sensibility*. It is to be regretted that, in the interests of the plot, she tries to deceive the reader (and possibly deceives herself) into giving the prejudice against Darcy too great a causal importance.

Elizabeth's discontent with Bingley, her regret that Wickham is not in a position to marry as he likes, do indeed connect with her 'prejudice' against Darcy (though he cannot be blamed for Charlotte's behaviour); her peevishness and spite come out at Hunsford, when she first sees Anne de Bourgh: "I like her appearance. . . . She looks sickly and cross.—Yes, she will do for him very well. She will make him a very proper wife."[42]

Life in Kent is empty and snobbish—as Jane Austen may sometimes have found it in another corner of that county. Colonel Fitzwilliam cheers her by his agreeable companionship and his evident admiration, but he tactlessly reveals to her that Darcy prides himself on having saved Bingley (if it were Bingley) from an imprudent marriage—obviously from marriage with Jane. Elizabeth's nervous distress results in 'agitation and tears' and a 'headache';[43] she sits at home alone, exacerbating her feelings further by a re-perusal of Jane's letters, and it is then that Darcy makes his proposal. She rejects him with 'petulance and acrimony'.[44]

After Darcy's letter, and her slow digestion of it, comes Elizabeth's awakening. "How despicably have I acted!" she cried.—"I, who have prided myself on my discernment!—I, who have valued myself on my abilities! who have often disdained the generous candour of my sister, and gratified my vanity, in useless or blameable distrust.—How humiliating is this discovery.—Yet, how just a humiliation! . . . Till this moment, I never knew myself."[45]

As she re-reads the letter, her social frustration also deepens; she has been well aware of the vulgarity of her mother and of the younger girls (like Marianne Dashwood, Elizabeth only has one sister—though her mother has other daughters), but it must be the first time that she has heard so frank an outside comment on it. 'She felt depressed beyond any thing she had ever known before.'[46] The impression remained with her: 'not a day went by without a solitary walk, in which she might indulge in all the delight of unpleasant recollections.' 'In her own past behaviour, there was a constant source of vexation and regret; and in the unhappy defects of her family a subject of yet heavier chagrin. They were hopeless of remedy.'[47]

Each of the four heroines who suffer 'awakening' is allowed comfort in a good and sound human relationship: Catherine is soon consoled by the affection of Henry and Eleanor Tilney, Emma by the love of Mr Knightley, Elizabeth (like Marianne before her) by sisterly love. "Oh! how I wanted you"![48] she cries to Jane.

Life at Longbourn has all its old tiresomenesses, and Elizabeth is even more painfully aware of the vulgar flirtatiousness of Kitty and Lydia, and the empty pretentiousness of Mary. (I am less convinced than some readers that Mary is a superfluous character. She is a mere dummy, of course; her relations with her father, a real intellectual, ought to have been developed. But she contributes to the intolerableness of the situation.)

Elizabeth tries to have a serious talk with her father, tries at least to persuade him to forbid the mad scheme of Lydia's visit to Brighton. Mr Bennet (for the sake of domestic peace) irresponsibly rejects her advice, and she is disappointed. 'It was not in her nature, however, to increase her vexations by dwelling on them. She was confident of having performed her duty, and to fret over unavoidable evils, or augment them by anxiety, was no part of her disposition.'[49] This moralizing piece of summary is not very satisfactory: Elizabeth had, indeed, a happy nature; but we have lately seen her in 'agitation and tears' over the past, and it is hard to believe that anxiety for the future could be so easily brushed aside.

The regiment goes, and Elizabeth has to endure the repinings of Kitty and her mother, and she is by no means without anxiety for Lydia. 'Upon the whole, therefore, she found, what has been sometimes found before, that an event to which she had looked forward with impatient desire, did not in taking place, bring all the satisfaction she had promised herself.'[50] She had to fix all her hopes on her tour with the Gardiners; 'and by again enjoying all the pleasure of anticipation, console herself for the present, and prepare for another disappointment'.

Elizabeth is badly in need of distraction from her own unpleasant recollections, and from the inelegance and intellectual poverty of her surroundings.

In Derbyshire she met Darcy again; he had obviously taken her words to heart, and touched her by his 'expression of general complaisance' and his 'improvement in manners'. She might feel that he was an example to herself. He now commanded her respect and esteem, and her gratitude: 'Gratitude not merely for having once loved her, but for loving her still well enough, to forgive all the petulance and acrimony of her manner in rejecting him.' . . .[52] And in this generous sentiment, all that remains of petulance and acrimony in her is now swallowed up.

§7. The Social Background

For the first time in Jane Austen's novels we encounter the country town. The Bennets' country house at Longbourn is only a mile from Meryton, and the young ladies are constantly walking in to 'pay their duty' to their Aunt Philips (married to an attorney, who had been clerk to their maternal grandfather, and succeeded to his business), 'and to a milliner's shop just over the way'.[53] They have more to do with Meryton than Emma, isolated by her invalid father and her own fastidiousness, has to do with Highbury, to which Hartfield 'in spite of its separate lawn and shrubberies and name, did really belong'.[54]

The neighbourhood is large, the Bennets 'dine with four and twenty families'.[55] Only three of these are named: the Gouldings of Haye Park, Mrs Long and her nieces, and the family of Sir William Lucas. Other houses are mentioned where some of these families may have lived: Purvis Lodge, the great house at Stoke, and Ashworth (though this last is ten miles off). Their closest intimates are the Lucases, whose father was in trade in Meryton, and knighted during his mayoralty there: 'the distinction had perhaps been felt too strongly'.[56] He is a pompous, common little man, with a wife 'not too clever to be a valuable neighbour to Mrs Bennet'. The Bennets' society is evidently drawn rather from Meryton (which is their mother's background) than from the county (which is their father's); this is inevitable, as she is far the more sociable of the two, and is without social ambition, apart from wishing for rich husbands for her daughters.

We see how their world strikes Miss Bingley (and it is before she has become jealous, so her testimony is not without value): "The insipidity and yet the noise; the nothingness and yet the self-importance of all these people!"[57] The fact that half an hour of Miss Bingley's company would be unendurable does not altogether discredit her evidence.

Many years later Fanny Knight (then Lady Knatchbull) wrote an extremely unlikeable letter to her daughter: 'They were not at all rich, and the people around, with whom they mixed, were not at all high bred. . . . Both the aunts [Cassandra and Jane] were brought up in the most complete ignorance of the World and its ways (I mean as to fashion &c) and if it had not been for Papa's marriage that brought them into Kent . . . they would have been, though no less clever and agreeable in themselves, very much below par as to good Society and its ways.'[58]

This might almost be Miss Bingley speaking, and it is hard to forgive Fanny for the snobbish and heartless phrase 'very much below par'. The letter carries with it a hint of how it may be interpreted; it was not Edward's marriage with Elizabeth Bridges that brought his sisters into Kent, so much as the antecedent fact that he was made heir to his distant cousins the Knights of Godmersham. Fanny's attribution of her aunts' 'improvement' to her father's marriage, suggests that the idea derived from her mother, and there are other indications that Elizabeth Austen was stand-offish to Edward's family—she may very well have told Fanny what she thought of her sisters-in-law when she first knew them, and before Fanny was born; one can hardly imagine Edward (so tender-hearted, and so devoted to Cassandra) doing such a thing.

In spite of Miss Bingley, and her female and feline strictures on Elizabeth and her 'most country town indifference to decorum',[59] we are meant to accept the more generous masculine view of Bingley and Darcy, even though they are in love with Jane and Elizabeth. "If they had uncles enough to fill *all* Cheapside, it would not make them one jot less agreeable". And (though the pomposity is worthy of Mr Collins): "But amidst your concern for the defects of your nearest relations . . . let it give you consolation to consider that, to have conducted yourselves so as to avoid any share of the like censure, is praise no less generally bestowed on you and your eldest sister, than it is honourable to the sense and disposition of both."[61] Darcy, even (though this may be a lover's partiality), is far from finding in Elizabeth 'the most complete ignorance of the World and its ways.' "*You* cannot have a right to such very strong local attachment. *You* cannot have been always at Longbourn."[62] The final word, however, may be that of Mr Bennet; he knows what he is talking about. Even Lady Catherine accepts him as a gentleman, and he is entirely free from parental partiality for his sillier daughters: "Wherever you and Jane are known, you must be respected and valued."[63] And so, one is convinced, must have been Cassandra and Jane Austen.

Jane Austen's situation, of course, was different from that of Elizabeth Bennet; though she had no Longbourn House for a background, she had no silly younger sisters, no uncles in trade and no aunts married to country town attorneys. None of her closer connections belonged to a lower order than the country clergy, a class now better considered than it had been in Fielding's time: three of Elizabeth Austen's younger brothers were members of it, while her sister Harriot ('the *bru* of *feu* the Archbishop')[64] married a clergyman, who was the son of an Archbishop of Canterbury who had himself been the son of a butcher in Gloucester.

Nevertheless, her Hampshire background was somewhat obscure, and the snobbery of relations by marriage who looked down on her and Cassandra, small thing though it may have been, may well have hurt them. More important was the struggle that must have been theirs, to achieve and maintain a refinement of mind and manners, while living as acceptable members of a provincial society, and not being too grand for the Basingstoke balls. Mr E. M. Forster, in his unfortunate review of the Letters, thought that, in the early years, it was Lydia Bennet who held the pen; they are much more like letters that Elizabeth Bennet might have written to Jane.

If Jane Austen acquiesced, sensibly enough, in the world in which she lived and of which she wrote, nothing could be shallower than to suppose that it had her uncritical approval.

'To be sure it would have been more for the advantage of conversation, had Miss Lydia Bennet come upon the town; or, as the happiest alternative, been secluded from the world, in some distant farm house. But there was much to be talked of, in marrying her; and the good-natured wishes for her well-doing, which had proceeded before, from all the spiteful old ladies in Meryton, lost but little of their spirit in this change of circumstances, because with such a husband, her misery was considered certain.'[65] Here is a note of the same bitterness as that in Henry Tilney's remark: "Every man is surrounded by a neighbourhood of voluntary spies."[66]

The charge of provinciality against Jane Austen would only be of consequence if it could be maintained that she was uncritical of the provincial background (which we have already seen to be false), or that she was unqualified to describe the elegance and refinement that, in many cases, she professes to describe. Questions about manners, which change so quickly, can only be answered by a contemporary; there is no contemporary evidence against her like that of Lady Mary Wortley Montagu against Richardson's pictures of high life. 'Yes, my love, it is very true that Aunt Jane from various circumstances was not so *refined* as she ought to have been from her *talent*, and if she had lived 50 years later she would have been in many respects more suitable to *our* more refined tastes'—here Fanny Knatchbull is not so much condemning her aunt as a whole past age, an age in which one might speak of drunkenness and of natural children. Above all, she is condemning herself. 'From various circumstances'—in that saving phrase one understands: 'as she was your grandfather's sister, she was, of course, *born* a lady; but those Hampshire surroundings, my love!'

What may have been the personal authority of Mrs Pole I do not know, but she is a contemporary (not a mid-Victorian) speaking on a subject to which she had evidently given thought, and she carries conviction. 'There is a particular satisfaction in reading all Miss A—s works—they are so evidently written by a Gentlewoman—most Novellists fail & betray themselves in attempting to describe familiar scenes in high Life, some little vulgarism escapes & shews that they are not experimentally acquainted with what they describe, but here it is quite different. Everything is natural, & the situations & incidents are told in a manner which clearly evinces the Writer to *belong* to the Society whose Manners she so ably delineates.'[67]

Jane Austen *belonged*; the most that can be granted to Fanny (and her letter is particularly odious, when we remember the beautiful letters that Jane Austen wrote to her, when chosen as her confidante), is that her aunt was never smart, a thing that no English man or woman of genius has perhaps yet been. Smartness is, of course, not necessarily incompatible with talent, though the pursuit of it has been fatal to a great many talented persons.

§8. Irony

Pride and Prejudice and *Emma* are Jane Austen's great detective novels; in *Emma* the underlying mystery is kept up longer, but the plot of *Pride and Prejudice*, till the moment of Darcy's declaration, affords even more wonderful opportunity for irony and misunderstanding.

In both these novels there is a small introductory comedy: the tale of Harriet Smith and Mr Elton, and that of Charlotte Lucas and Mr Collins.

These two 'curtain-raisers' are oddly antithetical: Emma fills her silly confidante, Harriet, with romantic ideas about a gushing young clergyman, who proves to be attached to herself. Elizabeth complains to her sensible confidante about a pompous young clergyman who is paying her his addresses, and Charlotte quietly annexes him.

At the Netherfield ball, Elizabeth pointed out Mr Collins to Charlotte's 'particular notice';[68] and later on in the evening 'She owed her greatest relief to her friend Miss Lucas, who often joined

49

them, and goodnaturedly engaged Mr Collins's conversation to herself.'[69] The next morning Charlotte came to Longbourn, to spend the day and (no doubt) talk over the ball; she arrived to find the family in confusion, after Elizabeth's rejection of Mr Collins. Mr Collins now left Elizabeth alone, 'and the assiduous attentions which he had been so sensible of himself, were transferred for the rest of the day to Miss Lucas, whose civility in listening to him, was a seasonable relief to them all, and especially to her friend'.[70] It soon appeared that, in spite of Elizabeth's rejection of his addresses, he meant to stay on.

The next evening the Longbourn family dined at Lucas Lodge: 'and again during the chief of the day, was Miss Lucas so kind as to listen to Mr Collins'.[71] And now it is revealed to us that she schemes to secure his proposals to herself. Two days later the engagement is announced, privately by Charlotte to Elizabeth, and publicly by Sir William to the Bennet family. Charlotte has acted up to the cynical views on marriage which she had earlier expressed to Elizabeth, from whom she had provoked the reply: "It is not sound. You know it is not sound, and that you would never act in this way yourself."[72]

Mrs Leavis[73] wishes to derive the situation from that in *The Three Sisters* in *Volume the First*, where an unattractive suitor is passed from one sister to another; it may be that she is right, though this derivation a little reminds me of those people—with whom every novelist is familiar—who persist in deriving a person or incident in his work from one vaguely similar which happens to be known to them in 'real life', and of which he did not happen to be thinking. We do not know the whole of another mind's experience, and are too prone to give over-importance to the little we do know. She is on firmer ground when she connects the unsentimental Charlotte Lucas with the practical Charlotte Lutterell of *Lesley Castle*, than whom no one could 'make a better Pye'[74] (Charlotte Lucas was 'wanted about the mince pies'),[75] and when she relates them both to Charlotte in *The Sorrows of Werther*, who 'went on cutting bread and butter'. Charlotte seems, for Jane Austen, to be the name of an essentially unromantic person. Charlotte Heywood, in *Sanditon*, was 'a very sober-minded young lady'[76]—though by that time the name may have acquired a wider connotation: "I admire the Sagacity & Taste of Charlotte Williams [a friend of the Biggs of Manydown]. Those large dark eyes always judge well.—I will compliment her, by naming a Heroine after her."[77]

In her account of Darcy's growing attachment to Elizabeth, Jane Austen plays scrupulously fair; the reader has all the clues. At Lucas Lodge he noticed the intelligence of her dark eyes, he found 'her figure to be light and pleasing', and though 'her manners were not those of the fashionable world, he was caught by their easy playfulness'.[78] But if he had not believed himself to be perfectly indifferent, he would hardly have mentioned his admiration to Miss Bingley.

At Netherfield, during Jane's illness, Darcy's interest deepened; Elizabeth's intelligence and independence seemed all the more admirable, her pertness the more forgivable, in contrast with Miss Bingley's vapid flattery. The beautiful irony of one of these scenes should be enjoyable even on a first reading, though it is only on subsequent readings that all its implications are likely to be seized.

'After playing some Italian songs, Miss Bingley varied the charm by a lively Scotch air; and soon afterwards Mr Darcy, drawing near Elizabeth, said to her—

' "Do not you feel a great inclination, Miss Bennet, to seize such an opportunity of dancing a reel?"

'She smiled, but made no answer. He repeated the question, with some surprise at her silence.

' "Oh!" she said, "I heard you before; but I could not immediately determine what to say in reply. You wanted me, I know, to say 'Yes', that you might have the pleasure of despising my taste; but I always delight in overthrowing those kind of schemes, and cheating a person of their premeditated contempt; I have therefore made up my mind to tell you, that I do not want to dance a reel at all; and now despise me if you dare."

' "Indeed I do not dare."

'Elizabeth, having rather expected to affront him, was amazed at his gallantry; but there was a mixture of sweetness and archness in her manner which made it difficult for her to affront anybody; and Darcy had never been so bewitched by any woman as he was by her. He really believed, that were it not for the inferiority of her connections, he should be in some danger.'[79]

In a sensitive essay, Mr Reuben Brower commented on the inadequacy of any possible stage rendering of the scene (and, indeed, any perceptive reader of *Pride and Prejudice* who has seen

versions of this book on stage or screen will hardly wish to repeat
the experience): we hear, as in poetry, so much more with the
mind's ear than any one voice could render. 'Elizabeth', he wrote,
'hears his question as expressing "premeditated contempt" ' and
scorn of her own taste. But from Mr Darcy's next remark and the
comment which follows it and from his repeating his question and
showing "some surprise", we may hear in his request a tone ex-
pressive of some interest, perhaps only gallantry, perhaps, as
Elizabeth later puts it, "somewhat of a friendlier nature". We
could hear his "indeed I do not dare" as pure gallantry (Elizabeth's version) or as a sign of conventional "Marriage intentions"
(Miss Bingley's interpretation), if it were not for the nice reserva-
tion "He believed, that were it not for the inferiority of her connections, he should be in some danger." We must hear the remark
in a tone which includes this qualification.'[80]

Perhaps I may quote a comment of my own. 'Probably one
should go even further than Mr Brower: he seems to imply that
while Darcy's frame of mind was complex, Elizabeth shifted from
one simple point-of-view to another, and Miss Bingley's point-of-
view remained steady. It is likely that there was a good deal of
ambiguity in the ladies' minds. In consequence, in the mind's ear,
the attentive reader does not hear one voice, but a lovely polyphony of voices saying: "Indeed I do not dare." '[81] To read Jane
Austen for the surface story is about as intelligent as to listen to
a string quartet simply for the sake of the tunes.

Of course, Elizabeth, out of all that polyphony of voices, does
not catch the voice that she ought to hear. Her prejudice deepens,
as does Darcy's pride; he still so deeply misunderstands her (and
he will for five months more) that he is afraid of giving signs of
admiration that may 'elevate her with the hope of influencing his
felicity'[82]—much as he might otherwise enjoy teasing Miss Bingley.

Some ten days later, at the Netherfield ball, Sir William Lucas
drops a hint to Darcy that the neighbourhood is expecting a
marriage between Bingley and Jane Bennet; Darcy's own preoccupations may have prevented him from noticing anything in
that quarter, and Sir William is about the only person insensitive
enough to address him on such a subject. Mrs Hurst and Miss
Bingley prove to be equally uneasy on the subject, and Netherfield
is abandoned.

At Rosings, Elizabeth's superiority is again evident to Darcy;

and now the tables are turned. In Hertfordshire, Elizabeth had to blush for the impropriety of her family; in Kent Darcy must blush for the rudeness and ill-breeding of his. And, as at home Elizabeth had, in Jane, someone of whom she need never feel ashamed, so, in his aunt's house, Darcy is supported by the polite (if shadowy) Fitzwilliam.

Even in Hertfordshire (though some of the Netherfield conversation is rather jejune, and may well be early work), Darcy and Elizabeth had found some amusement in being sparring partners; but here Darcy's approach to friendship is evident, and is of a kind to reveal his character and to attach Elizabeth, were her prejudice less invincible. He admits to shyness and, very ingeniously, joins her (though she is far from shy) with himself, saying: "We neither of us perform to strangers."[83] Fitzwilliam reveals that they had been going to leave, and that Darcy had at least once put off their departure. Charlotte knows Elizabeth so little (she has lost some of her confidence by her sordid marriage) that only fear of disappointing her friend keeps her from dropping a hint: 'for in her opinion it admitted not of a doubt, that all her friend's dislike would vanish, if she could suppose him in her power'.[84] Poor Charlotte is sinking to her husband's level: 'Mr Darcy had considerable patronage in the church.'

Nevertheless, with all Darcy's nearer approach to likeableness and to Elizabeth, his proposal, however many times one reads the book, is always a shock, as it is meant to be; I believe that Darcy is more than half-conscious that he more than half wishes to be refused, and that Jane Austen is aware of this (though she sometimes seems to forget it, and Darcy and Elizabeth will later find it convenient to do so). In his arrogant proposal he states the case against Elizabeth as strongly as he possibly can. He can then forget it, and begin to turn towards her; his conversion to better manners is then by no means unnatural.

It is the writer's great excellence that, by manipulating character and incident and word till they are at the most telling, she can fill this most formal and patterned of novels with a pulsating life. It is perhaps intelligible that, having gone so far in this direction in *Pride and Prejudice*, she should wish, next time, to make a wholly new start.

§9. The Anti-hero

Of all the anti-heroes, Wickham is the most odious. It is, indeed, almost as remarkable that Elizabeth should attach herself to him, as that Emma should propose Mr Elton as an elegant husband for Harriet. They are both underbred, and in Wickham's case we are allowed to suppose that an extravagant and pretentious mother had counteracted the excellent education with which his godfather, Mr George Darcy, had provided him. It is, of course, possible to find explanations: it is known that women often have bad taste in men (as men in women). Neither Elizabeth nor Emma has seen much of the world; Elizabeth is misled by her shrewdness, and Emma (who is a particularly poor judge of character) has a great belief in her judgement. Nevertheless, the improbability should have been done away; not the least improbable thing is that these two flashy men should fail, for quite a number of chapters, to show themselves in their worst colours. For ill-breeding cannot be dissembled, like a vice, and flashiness has no wish to dissemble. It is not only Elizabeth who thinks Wickham charming.

As a liar, he is indeed extremely plausible, clever enough to tell a great deal of the truth, and to exploit a situation where all the sympathy will be on his side. In life, or on the stage, his 'countenance' might speak for him; I think his creator forgets that it can do nothing for him between the covers of a book, and that she ought, in some way, to have made it up to him.

On his elopement with Lydia, Jane Austen has simply failed (or declined) to use her imagination—as on Henry Crawford's with Maria Rushworth. Henry went off with her 'because he could not help it'[85]—which is absurd enough, but there had been trouble brewing with old Mrs Rushworth and her threatening maid. The best explanation Elizabeth can give herself (or us) of Wickham's conduct is that 'his flight was rendered necessary by distress of circumstances; and if that were the case, he was not the young man to resist an opportunity of having a companion'.[86] But a young man in distressed circumstances, who is fleeing them, and hoping to retrieve himself by a mercenary marriage in some other part of the country, is hardly likely to choose that moment to burden himself with a mistress for whom he has no great feeling.

Maria Rushworth might be difficult to shake off, and Henry Crawford had the instincts of a gentleman; Lydia Bennet would not have presented the same problem, and Wickham was inhibited by no such instincts.

Mansfield Park

§1. Its History

Mansfield Park, we are told, was begun about February 1811, and finished 'soon after June 1813'.[1] Much of the writing was, therefore, done concurrently with the 1811 recension of *Pride and Prejudice*. The book is not mentioned in any letter before 1813, when, on 24 January, the author writes from Chawton to her sister (then staying with James): 'Now I will try to write of something else, & it shall be a complete change of subject—ordination—I am glad to find your enquiries have ended so well. If you could discover whether Northamptonshire is a country of Hedgerows I should be glad again.'[2]

The letter suggests that work of considerable importance was to be done on the manuscript during the last five months—if Edmund's ordination had not, hitherto, been an important theme, and if Jane Austen were planning some kind of revelation in a hedgerow, analogous with Anne's involuntary eavesdropping in *Persuasion*.

It is not till March 1814[3] that we hear of Henry Austen reading the manuscript. The book was advertised by Egerton the publisher in the *Morning Chronicle* of 23 and 27 May, and was no doubt published immediately afterwards.[4]

§2. The Pre-history

(1) Eliza Hancock, daughter of Philadelphia, the only sister of Jane Austen's father, married the Comte de Feuillide, who was guillotined in 1794. At that time she returned to England, and took refuge at Stèventon; in 1797 she became the wife of Henry Austen.

'She was a clever woman, and highly accomplished, after the French rather than the English mode. . . . She also took the principal parts in the private theatricals in which the family several times indulged. . . . Jane was only twelve years old at the time of the earliest representations, and not more than fifteen when the last took place.'[5] The author of the *Memoir* therefore dates them from 1787–90; that is, during Eliza's first marriage. Mr J. H.

Hubback (a grandson of Sir Francis Austen) records that 'theatricals were resumed'[6] during her widowhood; he started the notion that Eliza had contributed to the character of Mary Crawford. 'Their elder brother, Henry, was again Eliza's co-adjutor in the play-acting, and the outcome was that he became her husband in 1797. It has been stated that her refusal of James Austen in her youth was on account of his being destined for the church, but this may be merely family tradition. . . . Henry Austen had also the wish to take orders before he fell in love with Eliza, but we hear no more of this until his actual ordination took place in 1816, three years after Eliza's life ended.'

As James was only sixteen when Eliza first married, he could not have made her an offer; if there is any truth in the family tradition, it must (as Mrs Leavis points out)[7] have been during his widowerhood (3 May 1795–17 January 1797) that he paid court to Eliza. He and Henry may therefore have been rivals. Miss C. Linklater Thomson[8] went so far as to identify James with Edmund Bertram.

Another family tradition connected Eliza de Feuillide with the central character in *Lady Susan*. This short work, in epistolary form, was written on paper with an 1805 watermark; the manuscript, however, is a fair copy, and we cannot be sure of the original date of composition, which may have been very much earlier.

Mrs Leavis, linking the two traditions, has tried with great ingenuity to show that *Lady Susan* is a prototype of *Mansfield Park*.[9] Eliza de Feuillide's, Lady Susan's and Mary Crawford's stories have a likeness of pattern: a very attractive woman, whose values are those of the capital, comes to a country place, where people have more 'heart', and her impact upon it causes a considerable upheaval. Lady Susan's attempts to enslave Reginald De Courcy are observed with anguish by his sister, Catherine Vernon; just as Edmund's enslavement by Mary Crawford is observed by Fanny, his more than sister. It is quite likely that Jane Austen may have been a pained witness of the captivation of her brother, Henry, to whom she was particularly close. Only shallow people will find merely Freudian reasons for a sister disliking her brother's marriage; any marriage, indeed, must give some degree of pain to anyone really close to either of the parties, and it is only the marriage of cheerful extroverts, whom no one deeply cares about, that can give unalloyed and universal pleasure.

No one, of course, can suppose that Eliza *is* Mary Crawford. The references to her in the Letters show some affection, and Jane Austen would certainly not have wished to give pain to Henry who, if volatile, was far from insensitive. She thought with 'grief and solicitude'[10] of his anguish at the death of their sister-in-law, Elizabeth, a death that ought not to have made undue demands on his fortitude. And within a year of his wife's death she put *Mansfield Park* into his hands, and he read it with pleasure.

The story of Lady Susan, no doubt, differed as far from the real story of Eliza as that of Mary Crawford differs from it. While admiring the ingenuity of Mrs Leavis, and accepting some of her conclusions, I hardly feel inclined to say that *Mansfield Park* derives from *Lady Susan*; it is truer (I think) to say that Jane Austen was now making a new assault on a hill which she had unsuccessfully attempted to climb before.

In *Lady Susan* the heroine, recently widowed, goes to stay at Churchill, the country house of her brother-in-law, Charles Vernon. During the earlier months of her widowhood she has visited at Langford, where her time has been employed in seducing the affections of her host, Manwaring, from his wife. She has also detached Sir James Martin (a rich, silly baronet) from Miss Manwaring; she does not, however, intend him for her own consumption, but as a husband for her daughter, Frederica.

At Churchill she amuses herself by trying to attach Reginald De Courcy, the brother of Mrs Vernon, a young man who has arrived full of prejudice against her; her progress in his affections is reported by herself to a London friend, Mrs Johnson, and by Catherine Vernon to her mother. Old Sir Reginald De Courcy, reading one of the letters to his wife, is filled with uneasiness; he addresses a solemn remonstrance to his son.

At this point, Lady Susan's daughter, Frederica, is expelled from Miss Summers' Academy in London, for attempting to run away; this she has done, because her mother has told her of her intention to marry her to Sir James. Her uncle, Charles Vernon, fetches her to Churchill. She is a timid girl, of excellent disposition and studious tastes; Catherine Vernon at once takes to her, and Frederica seems to be falling in love with Reginald.

Sir James Martin, a fool and a '*Rattle*', appears at Churchill. Frederica, who has been forbidden by her mother to mention the subject to her uncle and aunt, is driven to write a note to Reginald

De Courcy to implore him to use his influence over Lady Susan to extricate her from the threatened match. Reginald quarrels with Lady Susan, and prepares to leave Churchill.

Lady Susan manages to regain Reginald's trust, and Sir James is dismissed. She goes up to London, leaving Frederica at Churchill; one of her motives is to see her lover, Manwaring, who is there, and is dangerously jealous of Reginald De Courcy. The latter comes to London in pursuit of her, and, by her direction, calls on Mrs Johnson; Mrs Johnson is out, but Mrs Manwaring is in the house, come to complain of her husband and Lady Susan to Mr Johnson, who is her guardian. An *éclaircissement* takes place; Reginald is finally disillusioned. Lady Susan ultimately consoles herself with Sir James Martin as a second husband, and Frederica is left in the care of the Vernons, who intend her, in due course, to console Reginald.

At the end, the epistolary form is abandoned, and even mocked, in a summary conclusion: 'This Correspondence, by a meeting between some of the Parties & a separation between the others, could not, to the great detriment of the Post Office Revenue, be continued longer.'[11] Mrs Leavis[12] sees the work as a 'novelist's working draft', put together to preserve 'fruitful notes', and carelessly finished off; Miss Lascelles[13] thinks the letters may have been written at Steventon, and that the conclusion was 'added at some time nearer to the date of the fair copy, when Jane Austen had lost patience with the device of the novel-in-letters'.

It is, of course, impossible to know exactly how Jane Austen worked, and it is almost certain that she did more work upon paper than most writers, committing to it first thoughts that were not, in themselves, worth preservation. Nevertheless, *Lady Susan* is very unlike any other writer's 'working-draft'; it seems to me (and one can only record an impression) to be an interesting if unsatisfactory work, preserved because it was too good to throw away (though not good enough for any other purpose) and roughly finished off, because an unfinished work is apt to nag at an author until it is given some sort of conclusion. *Mansfield Park* is (among other things—and the other things are important) a re-exploration of the principal themes in *Lady Susan*, rather than a new recension of that work. With this distinction in view, we may follow the detective work of Mrs Leavis, and accept a number of her discoveries, while giving them a slightly different value or emphasis.

Fanny Price, she rightly points out, occupies the roles both of Frederica and of Catherine Vernon; she observes and deplores Edmund's entanglement both as a sister and as a lover. It is for the sake of putting her in that dual role that Jane Austen has told us more about her childhood, than she has about that of any other heroine. (We hear something of Emma's childhood in retrospect, but we do not meet her till she is twenty-one.)

Sir Reginald De Courcy (as his one letter shows) is as serious-minded as Sir Thomas Bertram, and a great deal more unworldly. Reginald, who has no gift for soft speech and is of an embarrassing integrity, has a good deal of Edmund Bertram in him.

Fanny's Cinderella role is derived by Mrs Leavis[14] from that of Maria Williams in 'Volume the Second'.[15] "There will be no occasion for your being very fine for I shant send the Carriage—If it rains you may take an umbrella—" such is Lady Greville's dinner invitation to Maria. In it we indeed hear the tones of Mrs Norris on the occasion of Fanny's dining at the Parsonage. Sir Thomas, however, orders the carriage; it is a symbol of Fanny's rise in the world, and marks an important point in her story. It is at that dinner party that Henry Crawford first begins to take an interest in her.

Mrs Norris's officiousness and 'notability' (which she shares with Lady Catherine de Bourgh) may owe a little to James Austen's second wife, the redoubtable 'Mrs J.A.' 'It will be an amusement to Mary to superintend their Household management, & abuse them [Ben and Anna Lefroy] for expense.'[16] If James escaped Mary Crawford to marry Mrs Norris, one cannot congratulate him.

Edmund Bertram may, not impossibly, owe something to James, whose son believed that he had had 'a large share in directing her reading and forming her taste'.[17] In later life the sympathy between them was far from perfect: 'I am sorry & angry that his Visits should not give one more pleasure; the company of so good & so clever a Man ought to be gratifying in itself;—but his Chat seems all forced, his Opinions on many points too much copied from his Wife's, & his time here is spent I think in walking about the House & banging on the doors, or ringing the bell for a glass of water.'[18] Mrs Leavis[19] points out Edmund's probable debt to Edgar Mandlebert, the high-minded and sententious hero of Fanny Burney's *Camilla* (whose pedagogic attitude to the heroine

is developed far more sympathetically in the character of Mr
Knightley in *Emma*).

Henry Austen (who in fact married Eliza) may, as Mrs Leavis
says, be a part contributor to the character of Henry Crawford.
She rightly sees his name as a clue, and finds a common quality
which we may call 'Henrician' in Henry Austen, Henry Tilney
and Henry Crawford. It was one of the names to which Jane and
Cassandra Austen seem to have given a definite connotation:
'They say his name is Henry', she writes of a dull young man visiting at Godmersham. 'A proof how unequally the gifts of Fortune
are bestowed.—I have seen many a John & Thomas much more
agreable.'[20] Henry Austen had 'great conversational powers, and
inherited from his father an eager and sanguine disposition'.[21] He
may have been very like Eliza, his cousin on his father's side of the
family, and marriage may have accentuated that likeness. They
might therefore have given Jane Austen a suggestion for the Crawford brother and sister, and she may have hoped that this change
round of relationships would help to throw dust in everyone's
eyes. Here we are in the realm of conjecture, but it is reasonable
enough.

Mrs Leavis's derivation[22] of the Bertram sisters from Margaret
and Matilda in *Lesley Castle* is more ingenious than convincing.
She sees a link in their stepmother, Lady Lesley, whose Christian
name was Susan, and who was, like Lady Susan, worldly and mali-
cious. Susan, however, was to Jane Austen a name empty of
connotation; for a time it seems to have been the name of Catherine
Morland. And the likeness is not otherwise great; Lady Lesley is
no intriguer (or has no occasion to be), and the comparison between the tall Miss Lesley's and their 'pretty little Mother-in-law'
does not seem to me to be the origin of so simple a piece of observation that Miss Crawford's beauty, since in quite a different style
from their own, did her no disservice with the Bertrams.

It is true that they do not belong to that part of the pattern of
Mansfield Park which is paralleled in *Lady Susan*, and which may be
thus diagrammatically set out:

(CHURCHILL)—MANSFIELD —'Heart'	LONDON—a smart and heart- less worldliness
(Sir Reginald) Sir Thomas	
(Reginald) Edmund	(Lady Susan) Mary Crawford
(Catherine)	

Vernon and Frederica)	Fanny	(Mrs Johnson)	Henry Crawford Mrs Fraser and Lady Stornoway

The values of the Bertram sisters are those of London rather than those of Mansfield; they are on the wrong side. But the fact that they have chosen the wrong side is of first importance to the development of another theme in *Mansfield Park*, that of Education. They are not put in simply to help fill out *Lady Susan* into a work on the scale of *Mansfield Park*, and it is almost unthinkable that a burlesque like *Lesley Castle* (written as a joke, and kept as a good joke) should have been resorted to as a quarry; it is not, one must say briefly, the way novelists work. Jane Austen was perfectly capable of creating young women based physically on a country house, and spiritually on London; such was Caroline Bingley, and such will be Elizabeth Elliot. Life, no doubt, gave her suggestions for such characters, and there is no need to search for their prototypes, of whom there may have been not a few, both in Hampshire and in Kent.

Nor does it seem necessary to turn Sir James Martin into James Rushworth; their lack of intelligence might be about equal but, though Rushworth, like Sir James, is 'No Solomon', his worst enemy could not call him a 'Rattle'.

Everyone is pretty much in agreement with Mrs Leavis about two traceable contributions of real life to *Mansfield Park*, which had no place in *Lady Susan*. One is the topaz cross and gold chain which Charles Austen bought for each of his sisters with his prize-money in 1801; turned into William Price's amber cross, and docked of its chain, it forms the central theme of one of the most exquisite movements in the whole story. And the shock of the elopement of Mrs Powlett, who had 'staid the Sacrament'[23] not long before, when Jane and Cassandra Austen last did so, no doubt stirred some of the feelings of horror which Fanny felt at Maria's flight with Henry Crawford. Jane Austen might be amused at adultery in the abstract, and even boasted of 'a very good eye at an Adulteress'[24] (where her distant connection Miss Twistleton was concerned), but would not have been at all amused at the adultery of someone whom she had lately seen at the altar.

Lady Bertram, another figure at Mansfield Park who has no prototype at Churchill, is, I believe, not without importance to the education theme; her daughters must have been neglected.

'Almost the only rule of conduct, the only piece of advice, which Fanny had ever received from her aunt in the course of eight years and a half' was that it was 'every young woman's duty to accept such a very unexceptionable offer'[25] as Henry Crawford's.

Mrs Leavis is certainly right in objecting to her shining 'in the epistolary line', [26] for she is far too indolent; she is probably right in her amusing conjecture that Lady Bertram's great insensibility to Sir Thomas's dangers in the West Indies and on his journey are a deliberate burlesque of Mrs Inchbald's Lady Elmwood (in *A Simple Story*) who was driven into dissipation by the tediousness of her husband's absence, on a visit to his West Indian estates.[27] Lady Bertram has much of Mrs Allen before her, and something of Mrs Musgrove after her; nevertheless, she has an individual voice of her own, which can be clearly recognized.

' "Mr Rushworth . . . if I were you, I would have a very pretty shrubbery. One likes to get out into a shrubbery in fine weather."[28]

' "I must just speak of it *once*, I told Sir Thomas I must *once*, and then I shall have done. . . . Humph—We certainly are a handsome family."[29]

'. . . "I will tell you what, I think you will have a theatre, some time or other, at your house in Norfolk. I mean when you are settled there. I do, indeed. I think you will fit up a theatre at your house in Norfolk." '[30]

The tone and rhythm are absolutely individual; Mrs Allen could not have made any of those speeches. It is a piece of real character creation. 'Lady Bertram did not think deeply, but, guided by Sir Thomas, she thought justly on all important points';[31] Mrs Allen never thought on any points more important than muslin.

*

(2) Such a consideration of the pre-history of *Mansfield Park* would be a waste of time were it not of use towards the criticism of the finished work in which there are such inconsistencies and difficulties that we must look where we can for an explanation. It may be that some of the material originally presented by life has shown recalcitrancy when it was to be moulded into art. It may be that some of the ideas and characters have passed through a previous incarnation (in *Lady Susan* or elsewhere) which has left traces on them of which they ought to have been rid. It may be that

personal experience has not always been sufficiently sublimated. When Fanny is snubbed by Mrs Norris, we do not feel that any snub the parson's daughter ever received has rankled; it is not quite so certain that the pain a sister felt in watching a favourite brother being 'taken in' has not left its wound, too deep for the author herself to be completely conscious of it.

Whether (as Mrs Leavis thinks) *Lady Susan* is a vestigial *Mansfield Park*, or (as I think) an important theme was there attempted which was later handled in the novel, and was almost central to it, this is not the whole story.

Sir Frank MacKinnon's investigation of the dates (accepted by Dr Chapman)[32] makes it virtually certain that the chronology of *Mansfield Park* is based on the almanac of 1808 and 1809; the ball at Mansfield taking place on Thursday 22 December 1808. There is therefore some probability that an important recension of the book was made at this time, and that the 1811–13 date is that of a final version. The final version evidently contained important changes (as is shown by Jane Austen's letter of January 1813, already cited); but if the chronology were fixed, so must have been the main outline of events.

Mrs Leavis[33] believes that the epistolary form was used in 1808–9. It is surprising that Jane Austen should have used this form at so late a date, going back to it after the (presumably) narrative *Susan*. Nor can I agree that (in comparison with *Sense and Sensibility* or *Pride and Prejudice*) much of the central action is told in letters or summaries of them—until Fanny goes to Portsmouth (which *may* be a device to separate her for purposes of correspondence) the only interesting letter-writing mentioned is that from Fanny to her brother William. Henry Crawford, we know, was no correspondent; the letters from Sir Thomas from Antigua, from Edmund from Peterborough, from Tom to the gamekeeper and to Edmund, and from Julia and 'dear Mrs Rushworth' from Brighton could have told us nothing we care to know. Mary Crawford, of course, might have kept up with her odious London friends, but it is not easy to see who else could have done much letter-writing. Mrs Leavis thinks the 'dimmed and distant effect' of much of this novel is due to its being retold from letters; but the vivid drama of the first volume, with the visit to Sotherton and the great play scenes, is far from dim and distant.

Fanny's visit to Portsmouth (though it makes a breach in the unity of place), can be otherwise accounted for; Jane Austen may have wished for an opportunity to express her dislike of town life and her longing for the country. She has done so unforgettably. The urge to do something new, the desire to extend her range, the wish to exhibit Fanny and Henry Crawford in an entirely different setting—in which she was consummately successful—might all be sufficient motives. Moreover, the only vital correspondence, that between Fanny and Mary Crawford, was assured by Mary's visit to London; there was no need for the author to banish Fanny from Mansfield Park, unless she had really wished to do so.

The end of the book, however, is very much in Mrs Leavis's favour. 'An old and most particular friend' of Sir Thomas, Mr Harding,[34] is first heard of (off the scene). His first letter gives warning of Maria's most indiscreet behaviour; his second, sent express (and also summarized) reports that she has left her husband's house. The whole progress of her affair with Henry Crawford is indirectly reported.

The existence of an epistolary version of this part of the book would do much to explain (though not to excuse) its clumsiness. Ultimately, whatever explanation we accept, we must remain inconsolable; we are left with the fact that (however she arrived at it) this great artist passed for publication pages of astonishing jejuneness and artificiality. The finishing off of the characters in the last chapter echoes the cynicism of *Lady Susan*. In that work, Reginald is to be 'finessed into an affection' for Frederica, which, 'allowing leisure for the conquest of his attachment to her Mother, for his abjuring all future attachments & detesting the Sex, might be reasonably looked for in the course of a Twelvemonth. Three Months might have done it in general, but Reginald's feelings were no less lasting than lively.'[35] In *Mansfield Park* the author makes one of her very rare first person appearances: 'I purposely abstain from dates on this occasion, that every one may be at liberty to fix their own, aware that the cure of unconquerable passions, and the transfer of unchanging attachments, must vary much as to time in different people.'[36] Jane Austen might finish *Lady Susan* how she would, and might wind up *Northanger Abbey* by bringing in 'the most charming young man in the world'[37] as a sort of *deus ex machina*; those works were not, as she left them, meant for our eyes, and their people do not matter to us as Fanny does. The love-story of Edmund and Fanny needed completion, in scene and not in summary, and for lack of this they have been eternally impoverished; they cannot live in the reader's affections like Elizabeth and Darcy, like Emma and Mr Knightley, like Anne and Captain Wentworth.

No explanation can entirely excuse, but I shall attempt a slightly different one. I feel that Jane Austen is unlikely to have returned to composition in epistolary form as late as 1808, even though she might (and did) re-copy *Lady Susan* about 1805. And yet she may have borrowed some of the worst features of the form, the summary of implied letters, as a way of removing herself as far as possible from a subject that she found so distasteful that she might have done better not to treat it. 'Let other pens dwell on guilt and misery'[38]—and she should have let them. Mr Harding's pen will not do, for it is her own.

Her subject and the development of her characters carry her outside her (very considerable) moral range, and still further outside the much narrower range of Fanny's sympathy, and Fanny is the standard and the observer. She tidies up in a rather careless fashion (perhaps she can hardly do better)—a peevish and irreverent critic might almost say that a prim, evangelical spinster is tidying up after rather a disreputable party that she ought not to have given. This would be ungrateful criticism; we have enjoyed so much of the party. For once (and I think exulting in her new-found power as a narrative and not an epistolary novelist) she has let herself be tempted to the extreme limits of her range, and even a little beyond them. Perfection has gone by the board, and art has been sacrificed to life; it is understandable that this novel should show more blemishes and call forth more criticism than any other of her works, and also that it should be a favourite with many of her most judicious admirers. Next time she returned to her own sphere, and the achieved perfection of *Emma*.

§3. The Crawfords

Delving into origins may possibly help us, but we can certainly be helped by literary criticism, and that of the simplest. The earliest recorded (and it evidently gratified Jane Austen) was that of her brother Henry. 'He admires H. Crawford: I mean properly, as a clever, pleasant man.'[39] Thus, then, was Henry Crawford meant to be admired, and, to a large extent, his sister's impression on the reader must be involved with his. A few days later Jane Austen tells Cassandra: 'Henry has this moment said that he likes my M.P. better & better; he is in the 3ᵈ volume. I believe *now* he has changed his mind as to foreseeing the end; he said yesterday, at least, that he defied anybody to say whether H.C. would be reformed, or would forget Fanny in a fortnight.'[40] Evidently suspense was one of the effects at which Jane Austen was aiming; we are apt to forget, in a thirtieth reading of *Mansfield Park*, that it has to be read by everyone for a first time.

From these two points (made by Henry Austen) we can conclude that Jane Austen wished to explore the extreme possibilities of the Crawfords for good and evil; they cannot always (or even very often) act from the centre of their characters. Sometimes they go a little too far for probability and Art, even if they do not (perhaps) transgress possibility and Life. Moreover, they are presented to us not only as they appear to Fanny, but also more objectively. Miss Lascelles observes: 'The scenes between Henry and Mary Crawford and Mrs Grant lie quite outside the plan of her other novels.'[41] I am not quite sure what she can mean; Emma is spoken about by Mrs Weston and Mr Knightley behind her back —but it is one of her rare sacrifices of the unity of point-of-view. All this helps to account for the puzzling picture they present to us.

They are both victims of a faulty upbringing, and thus provide further illustration of the central theme of the book: Henry has been brought up by the immoral Admiral, and Mary by his wife, whose indelicacy of mind is rightly detected by Fanny.[42] Nevertheless, they are both able to admire goodness and simplicity when they see it, and their need for it is not without pathos.

Henry says of Fanny: "I could so wholly and absolutely confide in her . . . and *that* is what I want."[43] Mary says to Fanny: "You all give me a feeling of being able to trust and confide in you; which, in common intercourse, one knows nothing of."[44]

Their good humour and good manners are unshakeable, and their 'politeness of the heart' has a moral value. The arrival of this good-tempered and unselfish brother and sister who, 'late and dark and dirty as it was, could not help coming',[45] transforms the atmosphere at Mansfield Park, where the (no doubt) equally well-bred young people are sunk in selfishness and crossness. The Crawfords are ready to do anything, to take any part; if the play scheme has any impropriety on the score of Maria's engagement and Sir Thomas's certain disapproval, it is no responsibility of theirs.

They have a wisdom of the heart too, which results, at times, in great beauty of behaviour; the pure in heart, who are not so wise, do not always behave so well. Mrs Norris snubbed Fanny cruelly for her unwillingness to take part in the play. 'Edmund was too angry to speak',[46] and it was Mary who soothed her with 'a kind low whisper', and protected her from further molestation. Edmund, when he came to Portsmouth, was completely self-absorbed, and took no notice of anyone but Fanny. It is easy to imagine him, in later life, 'walking about the House, & banging on doors', and constantly 'ringing the bell for a glass of water'. He had not the considerateness of Henry Crawford, who could prompt even Mr Price to manners that were 'more than passable';[47] indeed, if one were asked to name an ideal good-hearted gentleman in fiction, one might think first of Henry Crawford during this visit.

Some critics have maintained that the flashiness and unworthiness of the Crawfords is obvious from the first, and that there is no real suspense; Jane Austen would certainly not have taken this as a compliment. It may be that she has been unsteady of hand when drawing them (and we shall have something to say of her animus against Mary); she needs to show their furthest resources for good and evil, a difficult thing to do.

Henry's 'sense' is frequently mentioned, and the author, speaking of Mary, refers to 'the really good feelings by which she was almost purely governed'.[48] Finally, we are told of Henry: 'Would he have persevered, and uprightly, Fanny must have been his reward.'[49] Some readers recoil from this judgement in shocked disbelief; but it rests on the authority of her who made Henry and Fanny.

I do not think it is frequently enough observed that, in the Crawfords, Jane Austen has bitten off rather more than she can chew; in no other novel has she depicted smart, worldly people who matter emotionally to the reader. Much of their conduct she can, and does, beautifully depict; but when she tries to realize other parts of their lives, we are conscious of hollowness.

Henry never speaks amiss, but the author's comments on him are sometimes at fault; Jane Austen cannot write untruthfully without also writing badly (a further proof of her integrity), and she falls into what she once called 'such thorough novel slang—

68

and so old, that I dare say Adam met with it in the first novel he opened'.[50] Henry found that the Bertram sisters were 'an amusement to his sated mind';[51] 'in all the riot of his gratifications'[52] private theatricals were yet to him 'an untasted pleasure'. And, in the final summing up, we are told that he had 'indulged in the freaks of a cold-blooded vanity a little too long'.[53] 'I do not object to the Thing, but I cannot bear the expression'[54]—so Jane Austen might have commented, had it been a niece writing. But the fault of the expression is that the Thing has not been clearly and distinctly imagined.

Mary, on the other hand, is condemned out of her own mouth. "Sad, sad girl!"[55] she says, and the stupid slang stamps her as Isabella Thorpe's sister, at the moment when she is aspiring to be Fanny's. And yet, she is a mystery; a few minutes later her words have the very rhythm of sensibility and sincerity: "for as to scolding you, Fanny, which I came fully intending to do, I have not the heart for it when it comes to the point; . . . Good, gentle Fanny! When I think of this being the last time of seeing you; for I do not know how long—I feel it quite impossible to do any thing but love you."[56] They never met again.

It is when Mary begins to talk about her London friends that her sincerity vanishes; something of the silliness of Lydia Bennet is heard in the voice of this woman, her elder in years and infinitely her superior in mind.

"Mrs Fraser has been my intimate friend for years. But I have not the least inclination to go near her. . . . And when I have done with her, I must go to her sister, Lady Stornaway, because *she* was rather my most particular friend of the two; but I have not cared much for *her* these three years."[57] And she rattles on heartlessly, but with another pause for sensibility—and again it is *confidence* that she praises. "Even Dr Grant does shew a thorough confidence in my sister, and a certain consideration for her judgment, which makes one feel there *is* attachment."[58] And the total effect of the meeting is kind and amiable; Mary shows strong sisterly affection, warmly urges her brother's suit (though he might, from a worldly point-of-view do far better for himself), and yet tenderly spares Fanny as much as she can, and earns her gratitude.

It is a baffling scene, open to several interpretations. Is Jane Austen failing in art, in her representation of Mary's worldly side, and, if this is so, is the failure due (1) to insufficient exercise of the imagination or (2) to animus against Mary = Lady Susan = Eliza? Or, on the contrary, is there an excess of sympathy, which makes Mary speak with heartfelt earnestness about those who have heart, and with flippancy about the frivolous? Is the sympathy (if this be the case) Mary's or the author's (that is to ask, is the effect consciously or unconsciously sought)? Or is Mary (who is not very happy, and not very much pleased with herself) attempting a travesty of the inferior part of herself, and of her life? I am almost certain that the last explanation of the scene cannot be entirely true of it as it stands (in spite of some wavering of the author towards it); but if it had been constructed on those lines, it might have had great beauty.

Mary's style in letter-writing is remarkably like Jane Austen's own, even to lapses in taste; her pun is no worse than some of her author's, and her 'three or four lines passionées'[59] no more tiresome than the little bits of French in some of the Letters, and far more forgivable than Fanny's happiness 'à-la-mortal, finely chequered'[60] or the dreadful 'con amore fraternal'[61] of her tears after William's departure.

The gaiety of her letter after Henry's visit to Portsmouth is entirely on the lines of several letters to Cassandra; and it is read by Fanny with an extreme lack of 'candour'. And in the imprudent letter, asking about Tom's chance of recovery, the words of sympathy: 'One should be a brute not to feel for the distress they are in',[62] are a strange echo of Jane Austen's letter to her brother Frank on their father's death: 'The loss of such a Parent must be felt, or we should be Brutes.'[63]

It is, of course, a mistake to allow Mary to apply to Fanny for news. Miss Lascelles[64] very well shows how Jane Austen directs our attention to the Grants' absence in Bath, to prepare us for this application. Edmund mentions it, in passing, in his letter; it would not be natural for him to make much of it, so it is underlined by an affectionate joke about his mother: 'your aunt seems to feel out of luck that such an article of Mansfield news should fall to my pen instead of her's.'[65] There follow some remarks on Lady Bertram's 'creditable, amplifying style', and we can never forget that the Grants are gone. 'Had the Grants been at home, I would not have troubled you', writes Mary.[66] Jane Austen has done all that she can to justify her blunder, but a blunder it remains.

Mary seems to be conscious of this; almost deliberately she puts her worst foot forward, and shows herself in a bad light. Perhaps, feeling self-consciously that Fanny will suspect her motives for interest in Tom's health, she tries to disarm her by making a joke of them; she ought to know very well that Fanny was not the right audience for such a joke. There is little evidence that Fanny has any sense of humour, and she is priggish enough to find any joke about death in deplorably bad taste, even if it were not about the possible death of a near relation of her own. Mary, and this is not without pathos, has rather too much confidence in Fanny, and is quite unsuspicious of her animus against herself, and of its motive. She has blundered badly, and it is now evident that Jane Austen is bent on her downfall.

Fanny's answer to this letter, refusing the Crawfords' offer to take her to Mansfield, is the height of disingenuousness. 'She must suppose her return would be unwelcome at present, and that she should be felt an incumbrance.'[67] She is telling a lie, and a quite unnecessary lie; she could easily have said that 'she did not chuse to return until Sir Thomas sent for her'. And yet Mary could easily swallow that lie, and put it down to Fanny's modest disposition that she could suppose her return an incumbrance, though it must be welcome to everyone at Mansfield except Mrs Norris.

Mary Crawford, indeed, lacked taste; she lacked 'moral taste' too. If Sir Thomas had been privy to her last conversation with Edmund 'he would not have wished her to belong to him, though her twenty thousand pounds had been forty'.[68] That is saying much, but not too much; Sir Thomas would have judged her as Edmund and Fanny did.

We need not think quite so ill of her; if a young woman speaks of adultery as 'folly', we need not be so 'uncandid' as to conclude that she does not also think it wicked. "No reluctance," cries Edmund to Fanny, "no horror, no feminine—shall I say? no modest loathings!"[69] And yet she spoke of Fanny with true affection, even though she made a little attempt at a jest.

' "Cruel!" said Fanny—"quite cruel! At such a moment to give way to gaiety and to speak with lightness, and to you! Absolute cruelty!" '[70]

Edmund did not put the speech down to cruelty. "The evil lies yet deeper" (how could it? an outraged reader is tempted to exclaim). "Her's are all faults of principle, Fanny, of blunted delicacy and a corrupted, vitiated mind."

Mary Crawford is a fictional character; she only exists when we see her or hear of her, and there can be no appeal against her creator's judgement of her. If we appeal against the judgement of Edmund and Fanny, it is perhaps casuistical, for they are the people who set the standards in this book. But we remember a younger Jane Austen who could refer with levity to the death of a first cousin.[71]

Moreover, we find inconsistencies between what Mary says and does, and what is said of her; we detect an animus against her, and both biography and *Quellengeschichte* help to account for this. And criticism suggests that Jane Austen has gone slightly beyond her range for once, and has tried to portray a character that she does not completely understand. It would be false and sentimental to say that there is more in Mary Crawford; there cannot be more than what the author has implied or stated. And the monstrous misrepresentation of Lady Catherine de Bourgh on stage and screen is a warning to anyone who thinks of playing about with Jane Austen's characters. Nevertheless, there may be room for creative criticism of the sort that (greatly daring) one might have addressed to the author had one read the book in manuscript. She has not done well in imitating her Creator by maddening whom she wishes to destroy; she would have done well to imitate him by hating nothing that she has made. She herself was generally aware of the necessity for greater sympathy with her characters; the trend of her work is almost always in this direction (as Proust's development was in the opposite direction).[72] If she could have liked Mary better (or if the love-hate see-saw had come down on the side of love), she might have explained the last scene in terms of generosity, of Mary's trying to let Edmund down lightly and to spare his feelings, as before she had spared Fanny's at their last meeting. As she has not done it, we may not; but we may wish that she had.

Like Willoughby, the Crawfords are, in a sense, ultimately saved. We are not told of Henry Crawford's amendment of life, but he is left with vexation and regret—'vexation that must rise sometimes to self-reproach, and regret to wretchedness'.[73] This is a movement of the heart in the right direction, and Jane Austen, who always liked him, need say no more. Mary is more handsomely treated (as if by way of amends); she finds a home with Mrs Grant, feeling the need for 'the true kindness of her sister's heart, and the rational tranquillity of her ways'.[74] She is still worldly, but she has 'better taste' (and it must include better 'moral taste'); she will not marry without 'a hope of domestic happiness'. It would have been gratifying if we had been told of the generous sympathy with which both the Crawfords heard of Edmund and Fanny's marriage.

The bright creatures have gone, and it is better so—Edmund and Fanny would have gone outside their true range had they married Mary and Henry. Mansfield Park is left to its quiet happiness and its humdrum virtues. But, indirectly, the Crawfords have done it one great service: they have caused the departure of Mrs Norris to that 'remote and private' hell,[75] where she and Maria Rushworth are shut up together, with their tempers for 'their mutual punishment'.

§4. The Visit to Sotherton

The bright creatures have gone; but while they were there they made Northamptonshire so sultry with passion that people stronger than Fanny might easily be knocked up. The first of the great movements in which they take part is the visit to Sotherton.

Mr Rushworth had lately visited a friend, Smith, who had lately had his own place, Compton, 'improved' by Repton; he came back to think Sotherton Court badly in need of improvement. His first thought was to have the avenue cut down.

Fanny had a sad, Cowperian feeling for the (probably) doomed avenue, and wished that she could see it, and also the whole place 'as it is now, in its old state'.[76] Her taste in landscape and architecture is literary and romantic; this is evinced by her famous quotation from *The Lay of the Last Minstrel*—her silliest and almost her most endearing speech. When they enter the chapel at Sotherton, 'Fanny's imagination had prepared her for something grander than a mere, spacious, oblong room, fitted up for the purpose of devotion.'[77] She had read of chapels full of tombs and (I think) was further confused between the words 'chapel' and 'chancel'.

Scott tells us of William of Deloraine and the monk of St Mary's aisle that

> *By a steel-clench'd postern door,*
> *They entered now the chancel tall. . . .*

But this was Melrose Abbey, and at midnight.

Fanny continues the quotation. ' "I am disappointed," said she, in a low voice to Edmund. "This is not my idea of a chapel. There is nothing awful here, nothing melancholy, nothing grand. Here are no aisles, no arches, no inscriptions, no banners. No banners, cousin, to be 'blown by the night-wind of Heaven'. No signs that 'a Scottish monarch sleeps below.' " '[78] This is the only occasion when we are invited to laugh heartily at Fanny.

But her interest in the avenue was only a small element in the excursion to Sotherton. Henry Crawford was praised by his sister, Mrs Grant, as an amateur improver; Mr Rushworth invited him over to Sotherton, to take a bed there, and give his advice. But 'Mrs Norris, as if reading in her two nieces' minds their little approbation of a plan which was to take Mr Crawford away'[79] (her ill-judged indulgence of them has almost turned her into a respectable bawd), suggests a family party. By the kindness of Edmund (who offers to take her place with his mother for the evening) Fanny is included; and Mrs Grant's good-natured offer to relieve him allows Edmund also to go.

Jane Austen has thus contrived the most splendid party of pleasure in literature: seven young people, all in love, or playing at it. They have an abundant collation ('much was ate');[80] they are exhausted by a tour of the great house under the prosy guidance of Mrs Rushworth; and when they are released into the open air, it is "insufferably hot".[81] As there are already enough reasons for jealousy and awkwardness between them, the resulting ill-temper and unhappiness are about as great as such things can be.

This triumphant movement has developed far from any epistolary prototype, if it ever had one; there are even reasons for thinking it was written into the last recension of the book as late as January 1813. 'Now I will try to write of something else, & it shall be a complete change of subject—ordination,' wrote Jane Austen in her letter of that date (already cited). It seems that it was then that she began to write the dispute on that subject between Edmund and Mary Crawford.

The seven young people may be (for our convenience) split into two groups; the trio, who carry the main story (Fanny, in love with Edmund, in love with Mary), and the quartet of the underplot (Rushworth, engaged to Maria, in love with Henry, who is flirting with both Julia and herself). They are worked in together with extreme skill. Maria and Rushworth stand beside each other in the chapel "exactly as if the ceremony were going to be performed,"[82] as Julia points out to Henry Crawford, perhaps not sorry to remind him of her sister's engagement. Henry plays up to the situation with two of his most 'meaning' remarks to Maria, and Julia (this time in innocence) runs to the other group and says: "My dear Edmund, if you were but in orders now, you might perform the ceremony directly." Mary Crawford, until this moment, knows nothing of his destined future, and she has just made a contemptuous reference to the clergy. Julia has upset several people considerably; it is fit that she should be left 'in a state of complete penance'[83] by the side of prosy Mrs Rushworth.

Edmund, Fanny and Mary now enter the enchanted wood, a small planted 'wilderness', and they go on talking about 'ordination'. They sit down on a comfortable-sized bench near the iron gates that end the path, and looking over a ha-ha into the park. Fanny, tired, and in danger of being "knocked-up", is left on the bench to await their return, and the other two stroll into the wilderness.

The other quartet (less Julia) now arrive. It is just possible that Jane Austen had thought of posting Fanny in a hedgerow at this point, for interesting overhearing (like that of Anne Elliot on the walk towards Winthrop). She was not sure if there were hedgerows in Northamptonshire, so she assembled the entire party on the bench.

The whole passage now takes on something of the character of a ballet: formal, artificial, and amazingly beautiful. The wilderness itself is a work of art, a planted wood, and none of the loves (except Fanny's) can yet be called genuine. Edmund was 'not yet so much in love as to measure distance, or reckon time, with feminine lawlessness';[84] Rushworth was merely formally betrothed. Henry was only a flirt, and the Bertram sisters were probably still safe, had they known their danger. Mary knew her danger, and was determined to be safe. And yet, by the end of this lovely, formal dance of the characters, only Henry Crawford remains heartwhole.

Mr Rushworth goes back to the house for the key to the iron gate, and now the dialogue emphasizes the stage-setting, which is symbolical as the background is in no other novel of Jane Austen's.

' "Yes, certainly the sun shines and the park looks very cheerful. But unluckily that iron gate, that ha-ha, give me a feeling of restraint and hardship. I cannot get out, as the starling said." As she spoke, and it was with expression, she walked to the gate; he followed her. "Mr Rushworth is so long fetching this key!" '85

We can believe that she spoke with expression, and her words are extremely poignant, though some of her intense feeling is disguised under the form of a quotation; but she sees herself as the caged bird in *A Sentimental Journey*.

' "And for the world you would not get out without the key and without Mr Rushworth's authority and protection" ', says Henry, pointing out how they might get out round the edge of the gate. And so, in spite of Fanny's protests, they do: it is a foreshowing of their future elopement.

Fanny is left alone, without sight or sound of any companion, till to her enters Julia, hot, out of breath and cross; she scrambles across the fence, and is soon hot in pursuit of her sister and Henry Crawford.

Five minutes after Julia's 'exit', and the theatrical word may be deliberate—the ballet in the wood near Sotherton being a forepiece to *Lovers' Vows*—Mr Rushworth appears. He and Fanny make an odd pair as companions in misfortune and jealousy.

' "In my opinion, these Crawfords are no addition at all. We did very well without them."

'A small sigh escaped Fanny here, and she did not know how to contradict him.'86

He dithers at the gate, and finally lets himself out.

The laugh of Mary Crawford is heard through the trees; she and Edmund return. They have found their way to the very avenue that Fanny had wished to see, and never had a glimpse of.

And so the day ends, and only Mrs Norris goes away the better for it—laden with a little heath, a cream cheese, and four pheasants' eggs. "There we went, and there we came home again; and what was done there is not to be told!"87

§5. *Lovers' Vows*

Edmund's aesthetic objections to private theatricals must be shared by most people except the performers. He likes to see "real acting, good hardened real acting", adding: "but I would hardly walk from this room to the next to look at the raw efforts of those who have not been bred to the trade."88

His moral objections have been thought to be priggish, but he has reason to call the plan at least 'injudicious'. "It would show great want of feeling on my father's account, absent as he is, and in some degree of constant danger"[89]—and 'the alarm of a French privateer'[90] on Sir Thomas's journey justifies this scruple. "And it would be imprudent, I think, with regard to Maria, whose situation is a very delicate one, considering every thing, extremely delicate." It is very much more delicate than he has any idea of, and events abundantly justify him; but what can he have meant at the time? Perhaps that she ought not to entertain the county at Mansfield before her father's return officially ratifies her engagement, and fixes a date for the wedding—although 'his most hearty concurrence'[91] had long ago been conveyed in a letter. Here, it may be, he is being a little fussy. He does not (oddly) advance at once the really final argument against the scheme, that each member of the Bertram family knows perfectly well that Sir Thomas would dislike it, and that they cannot be defended for thus taking advantage of his absence. Mrs Norris, who cares only for Maria's pleasure, eagerly collaborates in the scheme that is to make a total destruction of her happiness—and she gets some pickings out of it, including yards of good green baize.

Familiarity with the play is assumed; Jane Austen did not foresee how long the popularity of her novel would outlast that of Mrs Inchbald's work. She has not even told us what unmitigated rubbish *Lovers' Vows* is.

The following programme for the Mansfield theatricals may be of use.

BARON WILDENHAIM	The Hon. John Yates
COUNT CASSEL	Mr Rushworth
ANHALT	Mr Edmund Bertram
FREDERICK	Mr Henry Crawford
VERDUN the butler / COTTAGER	Mr Bertram
AGATHA FRIBURG	Miss Bertram
AMELIA WILDENHAIM	Miss Crawford
COTTAGER'S WIFE	Mrs Grant

Yates and Henry Crawford and Maria Bertram have got their tragic parts: the Baron, with his afflicted conscience; his wandering natural son; the wronged mother (whose 'situation' seemed to

Fanny 'so unfit to be expressed by any woman of modesty').[92] Tom has two small comic parts, and Mary Crawford (by the defection of Julia) is also to play comedy. Amelia's 'language' seems to Fanny as objectionable as Agatha's 'situation'; she has to make love to Anhalt, her tutor, and a clergyman. Against his conscience, Edmund allows himself to be persuaded into the part of the courted tutor, so that no one outside themselves may be brought in to act; Maria Bertram has engineered Henry into the part of Frederick, and he engineers her into that of Agatha, Frederick's seduced and deserted mother. The mother and son embrace each other a good deal, and it was well done of Mary to say to Mr Rushworth, to turn it off: "We shall have an excellent Agatha, there is something so *maternal* in her manner; so completely *maternal* in her voice and countenance."[93] Maria was probably about as 'maternal' as Jocasta.

As wonderful a situation has been contrived as the party to Sotherton; and we know it must end badly. Too many of the less worthy people are exultant. Tom has his company to manage, and his comic parts; Yates can rant to his heart's content; Henry Crawford and Maria indefatigably rehearse scenes of a dangerous tenderness; Mary Crawford has seen Edmund capitulate to her fascination, and against his conscience—"His sturdy spirit to bend as it did! Oh! it was sweet beyond expression."[94] It can come to no good; we watch the play scenes in *Mansfield Park* as tensely as those in *Hamlet*, and with greater anguish; the domestic grimness is nearer to our own experience.

There are two not very worthy people who are thoroughly unhappy. Julia is not greatly to be pitied; she could have had a good deal of amusement out of the part of Amelia, if she had not sulked. Rushworth, dressed up in fine clothes for the sacrifice, is also a victim to jealousy; and he has also the intolerable pain of mental exertion: he must learn his forty-two speeches. Fanny again is his only friend, as once before, in the fore-piece to this drama, in the *bois joli*.

> Il est passé par ici, le furet du bois, mesdames.
> Il est passé le furet du bois joli . . .

Rushworth has not escaped the cruel teeth.

Edmund is doing what he knows he should not, and Fanny has to prompt him and Mary Crawford in their love-scene. Edmund was 'behindhand with his part'[95] and it was he who wanted help.[96] Perhaps he wanted help in such a speech as this: "Why do you force from me, what it is villainous to own?—I love you more than life—Oh, Amelia! had we lived in those golden times, which the poets picture. . . ." Little wonder, if she closed the page and turned away.

The sisters are enemies; when not wrapped in silent gloom, Julia is noisily flirting with Yates. Maria is playing desperately for some intervention from Henry Crawford that will save her at the last from the Rushworth marriage. 'Maria felt her triumph, and pursued her purpose careless of Julia; and Julia could never see Maria distinguished by Henry Crawford, without trusting that it would create jealousy, and bring a public disturbance at last.'[97] Fanny (who fears a confidence from Rushworth) sees everything, and is alone in seeing it; the brothers are taken up with their own concerns, and Mrs Norris is busy with small economies on the costumes.

The first three acts are to be rehearsed. The Crawfords arrive, but without Mrs Grant, who is kept at home by her husband's caprice. Fanny is urged to take her place in the rehearsal, as Cottager's Wife; even Edmund appeals to her, and she cannot stand out. But a *deus ex machinâ* comes in the nick of time, to save her from guilty compliance. Julia, with a face all aghast, appears at the door, and utters one of the most dramatic speeches in all English fiction: "My father is come! He is in the hall at this moment."[98]

§6. William's Cross

The intense drama of the play scenes, and of the visit to Sotherton, do not at all look as if an epistolary novel were behind them; thereafter follow chapters in which the interest is more distant and muted. Jane Austen was afraid that, after Mrs Rushworth's marriage, her brother Henry had 'gone through the most entertaining part'.[99] And yet, within the third of these chapters, William is at Mansfield; Fanny has had no time to write many letters to him. It may also be doubted whether she would have confided the secrets of her heart and of Edmund's to a man—even to this beloved brother. (We know, from the novel as it now is, that she did not.)

The stages of Fanny's advancement in the world are carefully marked; Sir Thomas comes back to find her grown very pretty, and also to find that she is the only young person at Mansfield Park who has behaved properly in the matter of the play. She is also much the best listener to his traveller's tales,[100] even venturing a question about the slave trade, while his daughters show no interest. Presently the daughters depart, as bride and bride's maid to Brighton, and 'Fanny's consequence increased'.[101] The great mark of her rise in the world is her invitation to dine at the parsonage. Sir Thomas decides that she may go, for he concludes that 'all young people like to be together'[102]—and in Jane Austen's novels they observably do (and happy it is for us) in spite of what they suffer. I would not if I were they; and Fanny herself was not without some hesitation.

Mrs Norris (as we have seen) treats Fanny with a contempt like that of Lady Greville for Maria Williams—whether Jane Austen is thinking of her own early sketch or (as I believe) of the original experience behind it. The circumstance of the carriage is given its full value. Mrs Norris's spiteful attitude to Fanny and her jealousy of Mrs Grant; Sir Thomas's consideration for Fanny, and Fanny's 'changing status'[103] are all behind this incident, and Mrs Leavis rightly comments on its use 'in the one place and context where it will tell and do exactly what is required of it—it is this kind of ability that constitutes genius, rather than any more mysterious and inexplicable quality'.[104]

Henry Crawford has been away: it was 'early for Bath',[105] and it looks as if his sisters had sent him off,[106] till Maria and Rushworth were safely married. He reappears at the parsonage, and evidently falls in love with Fanny that evening.

At first he looks at her with the eye of an 'improver', and sees 'capabilities': "from what I observed of her eyes and mouth, I do not despair of their being capable of expression enough when she has any thing to express";[107] moreover (like Mr Darcy at Netherfield), he is fascinated by the one young woman at Mansfield Park who has been at no pains to fascinate him.

From the start we are told of Fanny 'that with so much tenderness of disposition, and so much taste as belonged to her', it was impossible that 'she could have escaped heart-whole from the courtship (though the courtship only of a fortnight) of such a man as Crawford, in spite of there being some previous ill-opinion of

him to be overcome, had not her affection been engaged elsewhere'.[108]

William came, and the deep love between the brother and
sister presented 'a picture which Henry Crawford had moral
taste enough to value. . . . Fanny's attractions increased—increased
two-fold—for the sensibility which beautified her complexion and
illumined her countenance, was an attraction in itself. He was no
longer in doubt of the capabilities of her heart. She had feeling,
genuine feeling.'[109] Henry now became aware of the seriousness
of his interest, and Sir Thomas (the most sensitive observer at
Mansfield) was also soon aware; Sir Thomas's awareness was, indeed, the final cause of the ball.

The ball at Mansfield produced the charming dilemma of
William's cross. William had sent her a very pretty amber cross
from Sicily, but, unlike Charles Austen (who bought 'gold chains
and Topaze crosses'[110] for his sisters with his prize-money), he
could not afford a chain. Could Fanny wear it on a ribbon at the
ball? Could she risk hurting William by not wearing it? To their
infinite credit, both Edmund and the Crawfords have understood
that it is not a question of dress, but of the feelings; by their sensitive kindness both hero and anti-hero deserve Fanny. The prettily
worked Crawford necklace, and Edmund's simple and neat chain
exactly show us the character of the donors. The necklace will not
go through the hole in the cross, and is worn as an ornament; the
cross is joined to the chain. This is almost a pledge to us that the
story will end as it does end.

Edmund, of course, does not see the Crawfords' (Mary Crawford's, it appears) action as rivalry, but as a delightful 'coincidence
of conduct'.[111] He is still pursuing a false gleam, and fleeing (even
ignoring) his true peace; this is a very tiring thing to do. At their
next great meeting on the stairs, it is Edmund for whom we are
sorry; Fanny, also tired, has the satisfaction of behaving with
extreme generosity—she accepts the sacrifice of Edmund to Mary
—nothing else will cost her so much again.

Virginia Woolf has commented beautifully, if rather oddly, on this
passage. There is a frail kind of happiness in this wonderful moment,
but surely too much pain for us to say that 'all the happiness of
life' is here collected. 'A dull young man is talking to a rather
weakly young woman on the stairs as they go up to dress for dinner,
with housemaids passing. But from triviality, from commonplace,

81

their words become suddenly full of meaning, and the moment for both one of the most memorable in their lives. It fills itself; it shines; it glows; it hangs before us, deep, trembling, serene for a second; next, the housemaid passes, and this drop, in which all the happiness of life has collected, gently subsides again to become part of the ebb and flow of ordinary existence.'[112] But if Virginia Woolf's analysis of the passage is open to criticism, her explanation of the beauty of such scenes as this demands our assent. She attributes it to the author's 'impeccable sense of human values', to her 'unerring heart', her 'unfailing good taste' and her 'almost stern morality'. One might add that Jane Austen is writing with her whole self, and with the totality of these qualities, and that she has contrived to make her dull young man and her weakly young woman fully present in the whole of their fictional selves.

§7. Portsmouth

Sir Thomas sent Fanny to Portsmouth as a 'medicinal Project'[113] upon her understanding that, by temporary removal from it, she might better appreciate the value of wealth and comfort, and, thus, of the establishment which Henry Crawford was offering her. Fanny thought that she was being sent for the pleasure of seeing her family, and of remaining a little longer with William. Mrs Leavis (as we saw) thought that she was isolated for the purpose of an epistolary novel. My own belief is that she went to Portsmouth chiefly because Jane Austen wished to 'try to write of something else', and that it should be 'a complete change of subject'.

As Edmund and Mary are both absent from Mansfield—he for much, and she for all of the time—Fanny need not have gone away to enjoy the doubtful blessing of their correspondence, and Lady Bertram's letters could hardly have been worth having. And both pride, and a resolution against complaining would have prevented Fanny from any interesting epistolary revelations of the discomforts and indignities of her father's house.

If Fanny had been one of Fanny Burney's heroines, she would have been overwhelmed by a rush of emotion at seeing her parents again. Jane Austen (who is always truthful about people whom she understands) shows her as overcome by noise and discomfort. Her misery is of a kind seldom well depicted in literature, though real and frequent in life: anyone who has been to a public school, or

82

who has done military service, or who (in the course of rough travel) has stayed in the worst inn's worst room, will at once recognize Fanny's experience—even to the expedient of sending out for biscuits and buns,[114] because the food is so disgusting.

Here, perhaps, Jane Austen is relieving her feelings by some exaggeration of the discomfort she had known in inns or lodgings, or had seen (possibly) in the houses of some of Frank's brother-officers in Southampton. Her sense of loss when living in a town is poignantly expressed in Fanny's nostalgia for Northamptonshire. 'It was sad to Fanny to lose all the pleasures of spring. She had not known before, what pleasures she *had* to lose in passing March and April in a town. She had not known before, how much the beginnings and progress of vegetation had delighted her.— What animation both of body and mind, she had derived from watching the advance of that season which cannot, in spite of its capriciousness, be unlovely, and seeing its increasing beauties, from the earliest flowers, in the warmest divisions of her aunt's garden, to the opening of leaves of her uncle's plantations, and the glory of his woods.—To be losing such pleasures was no trifle; to be losing them, because she was in the midst of closeness and noise, to have confinement, bad air, bad smells, substituted for liberty, freshness, fragrance, and verdure, was infinitely worse.'[115] Again: 'She felt that she had, indeed, been three months there; and the sun's rays falling strongly into the parlour, instead of cheering, made her still more melancholy; for sun-shine appeared to her a totally different thing in a town and in the country. Here, its power was only a glare, a stifling, sickly glare, serving but to bring forward stains and dirt that might otherwise have slept. There was neither health nor gaiety in sun-shine in a town.'[116] (Jane Austen herself, sometimes suffered from weak eyes,[117] and there seems to be a personal feeling in her reference to 'all the white glare of Bath'.[118])

Of Henry Crawford's delicate and beautiful behaviour at Portsmouth, something has already been said, and it may be added that Fanny behaves admirably on the occasion of his visit; her embarrassment never degenerates into false shame. We know and like both of them better for seeing them together in this new setting.

The sacrifice of unity of place has been rewarded by so many beauties, that it would require 'starched notions' indeed to blame it. A twentieth-century heroine, in the position of Fanny, might not improbably be thought unamiable for the complacency with which she leaves the Portsmouth family (except Susan) just as she found it, and returns with thankfulness to the comforts of Mansfield Park; but it would, I think, be anachronistic to expect her to entertain such scruples. At the end of the book (if we need such comfort) we learn that 'all assisting to advance each other' the Prices did very well, and were a credit to the 'countenance and aid'[119] of Sir Thomas.

§8. Education and Principles

Mrs Leavis rightly observes that in *Mansfield Park* the idea of 'principles' fills the place that 'candour' had taken in the construction of *Sense and Sensibility* and *Pride and Prejudice*.[120] Although Frederica Vernon in *Lady Susan* (like Oliver Twist later) is miraculously gifted with them, 'principles' are the result of education—a very much better aim than 'character', and one to which, one hopes, education is now returning. 'Principles', after all, are for both sexes, for all classes, and for home consumption; 'character' was only for the male sex and the upper classes, and was chiefly for export to India.

At Mansfield Park, it was the less privileged who were the more principled: Edmund had far better principles than Tom, Julia had slightly better principles than Maria, and they were all nothing at all compared with Fanny. A good and expensive education was provided for them all, but two of them learned only to be expensive.

Edmund and Fanny were protected by a prudential and utilitarian attitude on the part of their elders towards their probable future. Edmund was destined to a profession, and had to read at the university; a younger son who is idle and expensive at Oxford is not likely to remain there very long. Fanny was, 'without depressing her spirits too far', to be kept in remembrance that she was not a *Miss Bertram*',[121] and to be prepared for 'that mediocrity of condition which *seemed*' to be her 'lot'.[122] Moreover, Edmund and Fanny both had quiet dispositions which would keep them out of many dangers, and their fondness for reading ought further to strengthen their principles.

Above all, they were religious. Maria and Julia 'had been instructed theoretically in their religion, but never required to bring it into daily practice'.[123] Edmund, however, took his vocation seriously, and appears to have been under religious influence at Oxford.[124] Fanny was Edmund's pupil, and there is an indication that William was serious-minded[125]—Sir Francis Austen was spoken of as '*the* officer who kneeled at church'.[126]

Fanny had need of every available consolation to strengthen her against Mrs Norris—who made her character as surely as she ruined that of her cousins. Sir Thomas had left Mrs Norris's 'excessive indulgence and flattery'[127] of his daughters unchecked, hoping to counteract it by his own severity. 'He had but increased the evil, by teaching them to repress their spirits in his presence, and to make their real disposition unknown to him, and sending them for all their indulgences to a person who had been able to attach them only by the blindness of her affection, and the excess of her praise.' Fanny was the only young person at Mansfield Park whose education had been all of a piece.

Julia fared better than Maria, eloping to marriage and not adultery. We should have put this down merely to good luck, did not the author tell us that she had been 'less the darling of that very aunt, less flattered, and less spoilt. . . . She had been always used to think herself a little inferior to Maria. Her temper was naturally the easiest of the two, her feelings, though quick, were more controllable; and education had not given her so very hurtful a degree of self-consequence.'[128]

So far, the differing fates of the sisters looks too like the conventional conclusion of a moral tale. But we are told one thing very much in Julia's favour. 'She had had the merit of withdrawing herself' from Mr Rushworth's house when Henry Crawford's visits became frequent, 'in order to secure herself from being again too much attracted.' She shunned the heaven that led Maria to that hell; this was no mean merit.

The Crawfords had been spoilt by education; early orphaned, they were brought up by the immoral Admiral and his horrible wife (we are encouraged to infer that the latter, "whose knowledge of the world made her judgment looked up to by all the young people of her acquaintance",[129] had no very exalted principles). They had lived in a smart world, and with an example of unfaithfulness and domestic friction under their eyes. Their final undoing was due to a small lapse of Henry's; he selfishly remained in London, to go to a party, when he knew he ought to have gone to Everingham about his duties. And it was Mary who tempted him to stay.

Sir Thomas, 'a parent, and conscious of errors in his own conduct as a parent'[130] had much to suffer. He was more highly principled than Mr Bennet (at any rate, he had more to say about principle); but Maria Bertram's sin was worse than that of Lydia Bennet, and he was more to blame than Lydia's father had been. Mr Bennet had only been lazy and irresponsible: Sir Thomas had allowed Maria's hopeless marriage to take place, and 'in so doing he had sacrificed the right to the expedient, and been governed by motives of selfishness and worldly wisdom'.[131] Some of his anguish 'was never to be entirely done away'; Maria was a total loss. We may think that he shifted the responsibility for her off his shoulders a little too easily—not wishing to offer 'so great an insult to the neighbourhood'[132] as to have her at Mansfield, where she could not be ignored. We know too little about the neighbourhood to feel tender of its susceptibilities; Mansfield Park might be completely isolated. We are tempted to think (and are not much discouraged by the author) that the 'felicity' of getting rid of Mrs Norris leaves the balance so much in his favour, that Sir Thomas may well come 'almost to approve the evil which produced such a good'.[133]

Maria's life-punishment is a contemporary convention, though unaccompanied by 'remorse and a decline';[134] the company of Mrs Norris is a worse infliction. Is this 'supporting her by every encouragement to do right'?

§9. The Author's attitude

Sir Thomas, in the last chapter, receives almost as rough handling from his creator as that which subsequent critics have accorded him. His bitter reflections 'required some time to soften; but time will do almost everything'.[135] Time is as cynically invoked for the cure of Edmund's 'unconquerable passion'.[136] Jane Austen is, rather to our embarrassment, laughing at people whom she has presented for our esteem. She has said that she is 'impatient to restore every body, not greatly in fault themselves, to tolerable comfort, and to have done with all the rest';[137] and her impatience is a little too obvious. She should not, surely, like Thackeray, cry—

'Come, children, let us shut up the box and the puppets, for our play is played out.'

She is, of course, telling the strict truth: 'time will do almost everything'. Almost. Miss Compton-Burnett has told a deeper and sadder truth: 'Time has too much credit. . . . It is not a great healer. It is an indifferent and perfunctory one. Sometimes it does not heal at all. And sometimes when it seems to, no healing has been necessary.'[138]

We are not entirely wrong to feel ashamed of being healed by time, for the very worst things are never completely healed, and we do not like to admit that what we have suffered is not the very worst. Nevertheless, resignation is a duty (and Sir Thomas and Edmund, less religious in this respect than Marianne Dashwood, surprise us by not having thought more about it). Time does cause great and continuous pain to become intermittent and sub-acute— it has this advantage over Eternity. Reason asserts itself; if we were all heart—like dogs—we should die of grief as often as they do.

The process of recovery is gradual, and difficult to represent in art, and Jane Austen has confessed that she is 'impatient'. A small cousin of mine, whose father had been killed in the War, is said to have come down to breakfast on the day following the reception of the news, and, beaming round the table, to have observed: "We're getting over it nicely." This was thought to be 'rather soon', but the sentiment is human and right, though hard to express without an element of the absurd. I do not know that Jane Austen, or anyone else, has done very much better than the poor child.

I do not think that any of the charges of 'callousness' against Jane Austen can be made out. Mrs Hall of Sherborne's baby, Lady Bertram's epistolary enjoyment of Tom's illness, Mrs Musgrove's 'large fat sighings' over poor Dick . . . all these will shock few honest and observant people, and the objections made to them are sentimental or 'missish'. But, artistically, Edmund and Fanny do seem to call for longer and more sympathetic treatment than they receive.

Other objections against this book are but too well founded: the slight vein of priggishness, the clumsy ending, and the 'irreverence and oddity'[139] of the last chapter. Mrs Leavis[140] thinks the pre-history of this novel will 'enable' us to account for its anomalies, and it does help with the Crawford puzzle; but much is still perplexing. 'An artist cannot do any thing slovenly'[141]—and the end is slovenly.

That Fanny should be called 'my Fanny',[142] a distinction granted to no other heroine in the text of a novel, is understandable. The author has known her as a child, has brought her up—has known her jump about with her brother "when the hand-organ was in the street"[143]—Cleopatra, hopping 'forty paces through the public street', leaves some of us unmoved in comparison. And yet there are moments when Fanny seems to have stepped prematurely out of a novel of Dickens or Thackeray (except that she is too intelligent); she lacks vitality, and she is in danger of being a prig.

The vein of priggishness in this book is very strange; there is nothing of the sort in *Emma*. Mr and Mrs Cooke were 'very much pleased with it—particularly with the Manner in which the Clergy are treated'.[144] Whereas Mr Sherer, the vicar of Godmersham, was 'Displeased with my pictures of Clergymen' (in *Emma*),[145] and Mrs Wroughton 'Thought it wrong, in such times as these, to draw such Clergymen as M[r] Collins and M[r] Elton.'[146]

With diffidence I shall advance a conjecture. The expression 'a religious phase' is not one that a respectful admirer would care to use about a woman whose work and life and death were as consistently Christian as those of Jane Austen. One may however guess that she may have been going through a phase in her religion. There are signs that she was thinking about, and trying to make up her mind about the Evangelical movement at this time. Its 'enthusiasm' would be repellant to her, but its insistence on 'principle' must win her sympathy. (So I have seen serious people, revolted by the vulgar exhibitionism of the 'Oxford' Groups, but edified by the observable change for the better that they had made in several human lives.) 'I do not like the Evangelicals', she wrote to Cassandra, in January 1809;[147] 'I am by no means convinced that we ought not all to be Evangelicals, & am at least persuaded that they who are so from Reason and Feeling, must be happiest & safest', so she wrote to Fanny Knight in November 1814.[148] She was then writing *Emma*. I do not pretend to say where, for Jane Austen, the balance finally came down: I am inclined to think that she never quite made up her mind. She did not (September 1816) much like Mr Cooper's new sermons: 'They are fuller of Regeneration & Conversion than ever.'[149] And yet, in *Persuasion* it is solemnly objected to Mr Elliot 'that there had been bad habits; that Sunday-travelling had been a common thing'[150] (and no bones were made over Jane and Elizabeth Bennet returning from Netherfield to Longbourn on a Sunday).[151] I would hazard a guess, then (and with the more conviction because it is not only my own), that Evangelicalism was particularly interesting to Jane Austen during the last recension of *Mansfield Park*. (Mary Crawford uses its language: 'There may be some old woman at Thornton Lacey to be converted'[152]—Edmund was unlikely to have any heathens or notorious sinners among his parishioners, and the word must be used as Edward Cooper used it.) She was not quite sure what she thought of it, and in consequence was unsure in what she said.

Mansfield Park is a book in which she has tried new powers, has gone to the extreme limit of her wide range, and sometimes a little beyond it; a book in which she has made a new attack on an old problem, has failed to conquer an old animus, and has wrestled, not altogether victoriously, with a new prejudice. As a whole, the work has failed of perfection; but perfection, as Remy de Gourmont has written,[153] 'is only one of the qualities of the work of art, and there is a quality superior to perfection itself, and that is life'. There is more life in this book, and scenes of greater strength and beauty than anything else she had written up to this date, and it may be doubted if she ever surpassed the superb first volume. It remains one of the great novels in the English language.

Emma

§1. *Emma* and *The Watsons*

Emma was begun on 21 January 1814[1] and finished 29 March 1815.[2] It was probably published early in 1816.[3]

It is generally believed to be an entirely new work, whose rapid composition is attributed to the writer's growth in confidence and in practice. So cautious a scholar as Dr Chapman does, however, venture the statement that '*The Watsons* may with some plausibility be regarded as a sketch for *Emma*.'[4] Mrs Leavis[5] goes very much further—even (I think) a little too far—and her discussion of the subject is of great interest.

The fragment, named *The Watsons* by its first editor, was written not earlier than 1803 (as the water-marked paper proves). As it begins with a reference to 'Tuesday Octr ye 13th', it may well have been written in 1807. The manuscript, much corrected, and un-divided into chapters, seems to be a first draft;[6] its appearance, therefore, discourages belief in the somewhat dubious family tradition that the story was finished, and read aloud by Cassandra Austen to her nieces.[7] Her nephew, James Edward (who was brother to two of the nieces, and was helped by their recollections) knew nothing of a finished version, though he knew something of the 'intended story'.

He suggested[8] that Jane Austen did not continue the story, be-cause she realized '. . . the evil of having placed her heroine too low, in a position of poverty and obscurity, which, though not necessarily connected with vulgarity, has a sad tendency to degenerate into it'. Dr Chapman thinks it unlikely that she would have 'embarked upon the story without seeing where it would lead her'; but, before she had got very far with it, she may have realized how much low life she would want to introduce into *Mansfield Park*. There is low life in *Emma*, but we survey it from the vantage-point of the heroine.

In *The Watsons*, the heroine, Emma Watson, returns to a penuri-ous home at Stanton. She has been separated from her family for fourteen years, having been brought up by a rich aunt, who was expected to provide for her; that aunt has been widowed, has re-married (no doubt imprudently) and has gone with her second husband to Ireland. At present only Mr Watson (a widowed and invalidish clergyman) is at home, and the eldest daughter, Eliza-beth, a kindly gossiping woman, likely to remain unmarried. Emma goes to the assembly ball at the neighbouring town of D., under the care of the Edwards family. The ball is graced by the presence of a party from the Castle: Lord Osborne, his mother and sister, attended by Mr Howard (a clergyman), his widowed sister, Mrs Blake, and her small son, Charles. Tom Musgrave, a tuft-hunter and a lady-killer (though not devoid of charm) attaches himself to them. Miss Osborne has promised the first two dances to little Charles, but at the last minute she jilts him, in favour of a colonel. 'Emma did not think, or reflect;—she felt and acted—. "I shall be very happy to dance with you Sir, if you like it," said she, holding out her hand with the most unaffected good humour.' Her charming kindness makes her acquainted with the Castle party, particularly with Mr Howard and Mrs Blake. A consequence of this is a call paid by Lord Osborne and Tom Musgrave at Stanton, at the Watsons' early dinner hour. Some ten days later, Robert Watson, the elder brother, an attorney at Croydon, pays a visit with his wife Jane (who gives 'genteel parties'); they bring back Margaret Watson, who had gone to stay with them in the hope that her absence might make Tom Musgrave grow fonder. Margaret is peevish and fretful (another sister, Penelope, has gone to Chichester to hunt down a rich, old Dr Harding). Tom Mus-grave looks in while they are at tea, and joins them at cards.

Mrs Leavis observes that, summarized, *The Watsons* does not sound like *Emma*, but that nevertheless it reads like *Emma*—the similarity being in 'the tone of the setting' and in 'the details of character and intrigue'.[9] I am in so complete a general agreement with her that I fear my frequent disagreement over detail may appear more ungracious than I could wish.

Emma Watson, 'with an air of healthy vigour',[10] has certainly something of the appearance of Emma Woodhouse, "the complete picture of grownup health";[11] but her situation is given to Jane Fairfax, the secondary heroine of *Emma*, who leaves an elegant home for a poor household, and (for some reason) is not going to Ireland.

Jane Watson (who has a small daughter called Augusta) has

exactly the smart vulgarity of Augusta Elton, and her intended patronage of Emma Watson is transferred (and this requires some more contrivance by the author) to Jane Fairfax. I find it less easy to accept the change of Elizabeth Watson into Miss Bates (even if we admit that some twenty years more, and the function of being aunt and not elder sister to a heroine must make a difference); Elizabeth is gossippy and kindly (though very sharp about her sisters Penelope and Margaret), but she is motherless, and has no intention of remaining a spinster. Mrs Leavis is on safer ground when she derives the idiosyncrasies of Miss Bates from a Kentish acquaintance of Jane Austen's, Miss Milles, whose mother 'is chearful & grateful for what she is at the age of 90 & upwards',[12] who 'undertook in *three words* to give us the history of Mrs Scuda-more's reconciliation, and then talked on about it for half-an-hour',[13] and who occasioned the sad reflection that 'Single Women have a dreadful propensity for being poor.'[14]

The valetudinarian Mr Woodhouse, with his gruel, replaces the real invalid, Mr Watson, who was also addicted to gruel and cards. The sociable Mr Weston no doubt derives from Mr Edwards, with his whist club. And the Watson brothers, the attorney and the surgeon, find a place among the 'half-gentlemen'[15] of Highbury; the new Emma is elevated and removed from them. Hartfield, however, 'in spite of its separate lawn and shrubberies and name, did really belong'[16] to Highbury; it was not a country house (like Longbourn), it was hardly more a house in the country than Mr Tomlinson the Banker's 'newly erected House at the end of the Town with a Shrubbery & Sweep'.[17] The Watson world is at the Woodhouse gates.

Tom Musgrave does indeed pay empty attentions to Emma Watson, as Frank Churchill does (for a very different reason) to Emma Woodhouse; but I cannot believe that there is any real link between these very different characters. Tom's chief charac-teristic is toadying and snobbery, while Frank almost errs in the opposite direction: 'Of pride, indeed, there was, perhaps, scarcely enough. . .'.[18]

It is the assembly-ball at D., the high point in *The Watsons*, that makes a real contribution to *Emma*; Mrs Leavis[19] justly re-marks on the likeness of the ball at D. to the first ball in *Pride and Prejudice*, and the similarities between the party from Osborne Castle and that from Netherfield Park (though I cannot agree that

Lord Osborne is much like Mr Darcy). She well observes that Jane
Austen (in *Emma*) rejected all that was used in *Pride and Prejudice*,
and retained and beautifully worked up what was new—the
invitation to the dance.

It is true, indeed, that Emma Watson's charming kindness in
offering to dance with little Charles, hurt and humiliated by Miss
Osborne's selfish desertion, is developed into Mr Knightley's
chivalrous invitation to Harriet Smith, who has been abominably
slighted by Mr Elton. Emma Watson's action is the simple beginning of the plot; it introduces her to Mr Howard and the Osbornes
—it is almost a waste that such charming kindness should only
lead to an introduction that could easily be effected by other and
quite mechanical means, but Jane Austen was nothing if not
thrifty. Mr Knightley's kind action gives a twist to a story already
rich in developments.

But I believe that Mrs Leavis has only told us the half; Jane
Austen has been thriftier yet. She (who so often divided a character
into two—as Emma Watson, for instance, became both Emma
Woodhouse and Jane Fairfax) has made two invitations to the
dance out of this one, and the second is not the less important.

"I shall be very happy to dance with you Sir, if you like it," said
Emma Watson. Surely most readers of *The Watsons* will be re-
minded of the warm friendliness of the second Emma.

' "Whom are you going to dance with?" asked Mr Knightley.

'She hesitated a moment, and then replied, "With you, if you
will ask me."

' "Will you?" said he, offering his hand.

' "Indeed I will. You have shown that you can dance, and you
know we are not really so much brother and sister as to make it at
all improper."

' "Brother and sister! no, indeed." '[20]

§2. 'Brother and Sister'

Emma and Mr Knightley were not brother and sister, though
Highbury thought of them as almost being so. They were not even
within the forbidden degrees of affinity; his younger brother,
John, had married her elder sister, Isabella. But Emma's speech
shows that she came near to regarding him as a brother; and,

early in the book, Mr Knightley says to Mrs Weston: "Isabella does not seem more my sister."[21] He had played towards her the part of a mentor, not unlike that of Edgar Mandlebert or Edmund Bertram. "I could not think about you so much without doating on you, faults and all and by dint of fancying so many errors, have been in love with you ever since you were thirteen at least"[22]—so he says at the end of the story; but he did not discover his real feelings so very long before Emma discovered her own.

Emma is, among other things, a detective story, and I believe the pattern of the mystery may thus be briefly expressed: Highbury thinks Mr Knightley is her brother, but he is her future husband; Highbury thinks Frank Churchill is her future husband, but he is her brother.

Emma is connected with Mr Knightley by the marriage of John and Isabella; she is connected with Frank Churchill, because Mrs Weston is to each of them a second mother.

Brotherly love is an important theme in each of Jane Austen's novels. In *Northanger Abbey,* James and Catherine Morland are an affectionate brother and sister, while Henry and Eleanor Tilney are united by the deeper love that is often the consolation to children of unhappy homes. In *Sense and Sensibility,* as in *Pride and Prejudice* the love between the two sister-heroines is as good as such a thing can be in life or letters; but in the former there is also a kindly brother-and-sister feeling between Edward and Marianne, and in the latter Darcy's devotion to Georgiana. In *Mansfield Park* there are two mutually attached pairs of brother and sister, the Prices and the Crawfords. In *Persuasion,* Charles Musgrove is gentle and brotherly to Anne, and it is hardly kind of her to forget him (as in a finished version she might not have done) when she laments that she has 'nothing of respectability, of harmony, of goodwill to offer [Captain Wentworth] in return for all the worth and all the prompt welcome which met her in his brothers and sisters'.[23] We know what a good sister he had in Mrs Croft. I do not think this theme is absent from *Emma*.

Frank Churchill, who thought of Emma's penetration more as she desired than as she deserved, nearly made her his confidante at the end of his first visit to Highbury.[24] She believed that he was on the point of making her a declaration, and checked him, because she did not wish to hear it; he believed that she was, prudently, declining to share a secret.

This scene is almost acted out in reverse on the evening of the ball at the Crown.

' "How do you like Mrs Elton?" said Emma in a whisper.

' "Not at all."

' "You are ungrateful."

' "Ungrateful!—What do you mean?" Then changing from a frown to a smile

'—"No, do not tell me—I do not want to know what you mean." '[25]

'Emma could hardly understand him . . .'; she meant that he was ungrateful in not returning Mrs Elton's good opinion. He believed that she was telling him that he 'owed Mrs Elton gratitude for her attentions to Miss Fairfax',[26] and that this time it was he who was putting a stop to a confidential talk.

Emma, knowing that the Westons must have planned a match between her and Frank Churchill, and seeing herself so much distinguished by his attentions, tries hard to fancy that she is in love with him. She is extremely amusing; she talks like someone trying to persuade herself that an unsuccessful vaccination has 'taken', and need not be done again: "they say every body is in love once in their lives, and I shall be let off easily".[27] I suppose her here, as often elsewhere, to be unique in fiction.

On Frank's return, 'they seemed more like cheerful, easy friends, than lovers'.[28] Ironically, it is Frank who understands the real beauty of the relationship; Emma, always adorable, but always wrong-headed, fails to understand. Their silly gallantries are to him the play-acting of a brother and sister, impersonating lovers, to deceive the uninitiated—the very antithesis of the play-scenes in *Mansfield Park*, where two lovers play the part of mother and son.

Hot weather (which always has a deplorable effect on Jane Austen's characters) makes Frank overact his part; Emma plays up to him, and overacts hers, and has made all of us who love her blush with shame—there is nothing in all Comedy so painful as the scene on Box Hill. Frank Churchill, however, is most in the wrong, and he admits it: 'My manners to Miss W., in being unpleasant to Miss F., were highly blamable.'[29] He congratulates himself that Mrs Weston was absent that day, and we may be thankful for her sake that she was.

Frank Churchill, in his letter of explanation, speaks of his 'brotherly affection'[30] for Emma; he has always known of his feeling for her, has felt (rightly) that she returned it, and it has never occurred to him that she had mistaken his sentiments or her own. The pretence had been unkind to Jane Fairfax, and in itself rather indelicate, but the fun of it does much to justify it to the reader who (in spite of all the author tries to do) forgives Frank Churchill, and still feels chilled by the reserve of Jane Fairfax.

' "I am sure it was a source of high entertainment to you, to feel that you were taking us all in," ' says Emma.[31] ' "Perhaps I am the readier to suspect, because, to tell you the truth, I think it might have been some amusement to myself in the same situation. I think there is a little likeness between us." ' And in all their last meetings, they are entirely brother and sister.

Jane Austen did not (I think) intend a *lucus a non lucendo* when she gave Frank his name. Emma (in some anger at having been duped) cries: ' "So unlike what a man should be!—None of that upright integrity, that strict adherence to truth and principle, that disdain of trick and littleness, which a man should display in every transaction of his life" '[32]—and we know very well of what man she is thinking. But she would have felt very differently about a secret in which she herself shared. It was not a "system of hypocrisy and deceit"—and Frank's essential frankness is shown by the way he made a game of it.

But he owes his name, I think, to another cause. Jane Austen was, with reason, much attached to her brothers and sister; they had taught her the value of fraternal love, so beautifully hymned in *Mansfield Park*, and illustrated in each of her novels. And, I believe, each of them is there commemorated by name, in one of her fictional brothers and sisters. In *Pride and Prejudice*, the sisters are surely called after (Cassandra) Elizabeth and Jane Austen herself—though the characters are reversed. James (once Jemmy) the dark, melancholy clergyman, the student of romantic poetry, formerly her guide in literature, was always loved (though with exasperated feelings) even when ill-health had made him irritable, and he tended to repeat the opinions of his officious and jealous wife (who yet was a good woman, and a kind nurse). Edward (once Neddy) was her kindly host, a sweet-natured and tender-hearted person, and Cassandra's natural affinity in the family. Henry (once Harry) was Jane Austen's own natural affinity; a charming and amusing man, whose letters evidently do him so much less than justice. Charles was, to Jane Austen and her sister, 'our own particular little brother'.[33]

Their names are all borrowed (little else of them may be, though we saw 'Henrician' qualities both in Henry Tilney and Henry Crawford). I do not think Frank (Fly) has been missed out. There are not many 'Franciscan' characteristics in Frank Churchill —Frank was particularly distinguished as a disciplinarian—but one may be mentioned, 'deediness'. Frank Churchill was discovered 'most deedily occupied'[34] in mending Mrs Bates's spectacles. Jane Austen (I believe) only once uses this word again; of two of the young Knights she says: 'They amuse themselves very comfortably in the even^g—by netting; they are each about a rabbit net, & sit as deedily to it, side by side, as any two Uncle Franks could do.'[35] 'Deediness', and other features of the character of Frank Austen were reserved for fuller treatment in *Persuasion*.[36]

§3. Harriet and Mr Elton

This small fore-piece to the comedy is played out before the entrance of Frank Churchill and Jane Fairfax. It is (as we saw) a little like the story of Mr Collins told in reverse, but it is of far greater structural importance. Charlotte's marriage to Mr Collins is chiefly of use as a means of bringing Elizabeth into Kent; the story of Mr Elton and Harriet does very much more. From the start, it is wonderfully revealing of Emma's character. She is a romantic (and must be something of a novel-reader) for Harriet Smith's illegitimacy at once makes her seem interesting to her. She determines to save her from marriage with a yeoman-farmer, to improve her, and to make a match for her.

' "A young farmer, whether on horseback or on foot, is the very last sort of person to raise my curiosity. The yeomanry are precisely the order of people with whom I feel I can have nothing to do. A degree or two lower, and a creditable appearance might interest me; I might hope to be useful to their families in some way or other. But a farmer can need none of my help, and is therefore in one sense as much above my notice as in every other he is below it." '[37]

Had Emma been 'a degree or two higher'—had her father been a landowner—she would, like Mr Knightley, have felt that she could have something to do with a "respectable, intelligent gentleman-farmer".[38]

Mr Knightley is not only her superior in knowledge of the world, he is also her superior in penetration; he knows very well that the vicar "does not mean to throw himself away".[39] We are prepared for his subsequent penetration about Frank Churchill and Jane Fairfax—that is, the author is playing fair, and has given us a clue—even though Emma's obstinate self-confidence may bounce us into sharing her delusions.

Moreover, this first episode with Harriet is the first in the plot that, finally, will unite Emma and Mr Knightley. "Were you, your-self, ever to marry, she is the very woman for you",[40] says Emma, teasing him. When she had reason to fear that this unconscious prophecy might come true: 'It darted through her, with the speed of an arrow, that Mr Knightley must marry no one but herself!'[41] Harriet effects for Emma the service that Frank Churchill effects for Mr Knightley—the revelation of their true sentiment through jealousy.

The only awkwardness in this beautiful episode lies in the fact that Mr Elton should ever have been mistaken for a gentleman. "Elton is a very good sort of man, and a very respectable vicar of Highbury",[42] says Mr Knightley; he appears to behave rationally in men's society, and it is likely that he is good to the poor.[43] But Emma takes some time to find out the 'sort of parade in his speeches which was very apt to incline her to laugh'.[44] It seems incredible (though we know her motive) that she could ever have said: "I think a young man might be very safely recommended to take Mr Elton as a model."[45] His incumbency had already lasted a year, and he could hardly have failed, in that time, to betray the fact that, like the worthy Coles, he was 'only moderately genteel'.[46]

Marriage with the abominable Augusta Hawkins, who is vulgarly 'stylish' (whoever first applied that revolting word to her, has hit the mark) is his ruin, combined as it is with spite against Emma and Harriet. His meanest hour is at the Ball at the Crown. That scene, a postscript to the Elton-Harriet story, is a preface to all that follows. It is also some justification of snobbery (whether that of Emma or others); where heart and intelligence are wanting, it is a great protection to society that good-breeding should not also be absent.

§4. The Intrigue (I)

Frank Churchill and Jane Fairfax are of Highbury, though removed from it—he to be the heir of his uncle in Yorkshire, she to be brought up in Colonel Campbell's household. The theme of adoption has occurred in *Mansfield Park* and in *The Watsons*, and had occurred in the author's own life when her second brother, Edward, was adopted by his cousins, Mr and Mrs Knight of Godmersham.

It is known that these two young people have met, antecedently, at Weymouth; it is entirely unknown that there is a secret engagement between them. Leagued together, they converge upon Highbury at much the same time. She comes when the Campbells can spare her (they are going to their married daughter in Ireland); he, freer, though constrained by Mrs Churchill's whims, puts off his duty visit to coincide with her arrival.

Before Frank appears. Emma's creative mind has invented the Dixon story: Jane Fairfax has (she imagines) fallen in love with Mr Dixon, who has married her friend Miss Campbell, and perhaps he with her. It may be virtue (like Julia Bertram's) that prevents her going to Ireland; it may be someone's prohibition. Something is not quite right, however. Emma's conclusions (as usual) are false, but she has picked up one or two clues: it is odd that Jane Fairfax should choose to stay so long in Highbury, and she has a secret. Emma is so rash (and so disloyal to her sex) as to impart her suspicions to Frank Churchill—only when we realize that he is virtually her brother can we entirely forgive her. To him it is a clever device to conceal the truth from Emma, but very soon it comes to be a game that (he thinks) he is playing with her. Emma has been unwomanly, and Frank Churchill most indelicate; their high spirits carry it off, and Jane Austen earns forgiveness for them. Most unfairly, it is Jane Fairfax's repute that suffers; she is the kind of heroine who ought not to be 'talked about', and it is not logic but art that must restore her to our esteem, and this has not quite been done—she is finished off too much in summary, and too little in scene.

Emma, as Dr Chapman has observed, is very like the Jamesian spectator: 'We are hardly allowed to see anything except through the heroine's eyes; our vision is actually distorted by her faulty spectacles.'[47] Of Jane Fairfax my vision (at least) has been permanently distorted.

Dr Chapman comes near to accusing the author of breaking Crime Club rules, and wilfully deceiving the reader when Frank first calls at Highbury, with his father.

'A reasonable visit paid, Mr Weston began to move.—"He must be going. He had business at the Crown about his hay, and a great many errands for Mrs Weston at Ford's; but he need not hurry any body else." His son, too well bred to hear the hint, rose immediately also. . . .'[48]

Frank, of course, is longing to get into Highbury, and it is Emma who sees him as 'too well bred to hear the hint'; strictly speaking, we should perhaps be told that it is her mental observation, but as we are hearing through her ears we can hardly feel cheated. Off Frank goes, with an affectation of indifference, to see 'a family of the name of Fairfax'. I suppose most of us have, in our time, sought the deceptive safety of numbers, going to see 'a family of the name of Fairfax' or 'the Bateses'. Frank is unusually lucky in arousing no suspicions; Emma assures him that he will be struck by Jane's elegance, and Mr Woodhouse offers to send a servant to show him how to avoid the puddles in the street.

Emma is equally free from suspicion on their walk next day with Mrs Weston. She has no idea why Frank is so intensely interested in Highbury, nor why (seeing the ball-room at the Crown) he is 'very bent on dancing'. Her very natural enquiries about his acquaintance with Jane Fairfax at Weymouth drive him into Ford's shop to think out his answer under cover of buying a pair of gloves. It may be Jane Fairfax, and not his father, who has told him that it is 'the very shop that every body attends every day of their lives';[49] there is other evidence that her letters are full of Highbury gossip—one of the few sympathetic things about her. In the shop, Frank makes a splendid contribution to the Dixon story; Mr Dixon never cared for Miss Campbell's music if he could hear Jane Fairfax play. The scene ends with exquisite irony.

Emma says of Jane: "I never could attach myself to any one so completely reserved."

' "It is a most repulsive quality, indeed," said he. "Oftentimes very convenient, no doubt, but never pleasing. There is safety in reserve, but no attraction. One cannot love a reserved person."

' "Not till the reserve ceases towards oneself, and then the attraction may be the greater. . . . I have no reason to think ill of her—not the least—except that such extreme and perpetual cautiousness of word and manner, such a dread of giving a distinct idea about any body, is apt to suggest suspicions of there being something to conceal." '

'He perfectly agreed with her',[50] as well he might. Then they passed Mr Elton's house: 'If it were to be shared with the woman he loved, he could not think any man to be pitied for having that house.'[51] It was not much of a house; Emma was right that Frank's easiness to be pleased showed 'a very amiable inclination to settle early in life, and to marry, from worthy motives'. The sight of the vicar's yellow curtains, however, did not remind her of past folly, or prompt to present circumspection.

On the third day of his visit (which can be calculated to be Saturday) Frank Churchill goes up to London, on a sudden impulse, to have his hair cut. No doubt he has it cut, but he has another errand. At the Coles' dinner-party (which is certainly on Tuesday) we have the opportunity of guessing what it was, but I doubt if anyone, reading *Emma* for the first time, has ever done so. On the previous day (Monday), so we hear, a very elegant pianoforté arrived from Broadwood's for Jane Fairfax.

'That very dear part of Emma, her fancy, received an amusing supply',[52] she guessed that it was a gift from Mr Dixon, and imparted her guess to Frank Churchill. His conversation with her, when he allows her to persuade him, ends with the delightful irony: "I can see it in no other light than as an offering of love."[53]

After dinner Frank mentions to Emma that he had once been eager to travel, but was beginning no longer to have the same wish. She caught him staring at Jane Fairfax, and he pretended that he could not keep his eyes off her way of doing her hair. He would go and ask her if it were an Irish fashion, and Emma might observe if she coloured. He went, but, 'as he had improvidently placed himself exactly between them, exactly in front of Miss Fairfax, she could absolutely distinguish nothing'.[54]

Frank and Jane Fairfax sing together; Mr Knightley is 'among the most attentive'.[55] Emma wonders if there is anything in Mrs Weston's suspicion that he is falling in love with Jane; we may think that he is forming some suspicions of his own. An impromptu dance concludes the evening, and ends after the first two dances.

' "Perhaps it is as well," said Frank Churchill, as he attended Emma to her carriage. "I must have asked Miss Fairfax, and her languid dancing would not have agreed with me, after yours." '[56]

On the following day, Mrs Weston and Frank Churchill go to hear the pianoforté; he tells her that she absolutely promised to do so on the previous evening. He pretends to wish to get out of going himself, and allows his stepmother to persuade him. Presently Miss Bates comes into Ford's shop, to ask Emma and Harriet to join the party; she has brought Mrs Weston to add her persuasions, Frank being engaged in fastening the rivet on Mrs Bates's spectacles.

They enter the room to find Mrs Bates slumbering, Jane Fairfax with her back to them, intent on her pianoforté, and Frank with the spectacles. They have just taken up their positions, it appears.

' "This is a pleasure," said he, in rather a low voice, "coming at least ten minutes earlier than I calculated. You find me trying to be useful; tell me if you think I shall succeed." '[57] He evidently believes that Emma has guessed the secret.

The scene that follows can only be compared with the evening at Netherfield Park; if it loses, a little, in polyphonic richness, it gains in passion.

Frank pursues the subject of the pianoforté, and the conjecture that it is Colonel Campbell's gift, with an energy quite unjustified by the small acquaintance with Jane Fairfax, which is all that he has admitted. He is conscious of his words as a lover's teasing, addressed to Jane, and as a game shared with Emma who (he is almost convinced) is in the secret. Emma (little though she knows it) comes in for some affectionate, brotherly teasing about her Dixon myth. Emma takes his words as rather cruel wit, and as flattering to herself, who shares a secret with him—Jane hears them with 'a smile of secret delight',[58] and must be aware that Emma is believed to be in the know. Mrs Bates probably hears nothing at all. Miss Bates (if she is listening, and we are not told) will hear young people's nonsense, while Mrs Weston will be gratified to see Frank being very attentive to Emma.

Frank asks Jane to play one of the waltzes danced at the Coles'. "I believe you were glad we danced no longer; but I would have given worlds—all the worlds one ever has to give—for another half hour."[59] If there had been another half hour, he 'must have asked Miss Fairfax'; he has publicly and thoroughly unsaid what he said last night to Emma.

Jane played.

' "What felicity it is to hear a tune again which *has* made one happy!—If I mistake not that was danced at Weymouth."

'She looked up at him for a moment, coloured deeply, and played something else.'

We now have all the clues, and only the extraordinary vitality of Emma, the mistaken observer, could still delude us. A writer of detective fiction would be ill-advised to take *Emma* for a model unless he was sure that he could give his Dr Watson or his Captain Hastings her persuasiveness—a persuasiveness which can still cause a temporary 'suspension of disbelief' even at a thirtieth reading of the book.

Frank exclaims on the thoughtfulness of music being sent with the instrument: "I honour that part of the attention particularly; it shews it to have been so thoroughly from the heart. Nothing hastily done; nothing incomplete. True affection only could have prompted it."

It cannot occur to Frank that Emma can think him such a cad as (on her theory) he must appear to be. But of course Emma is very little in his thoughts, and he is talking for Jane to understand him.

Emma is reproachful.

' "You speak too plain. She must understand you."

' "I hope she does. I would have her understand me. I am not in the least ashamed of my meaning."

' "But really, I am half ashamed, and wish I had never taken up the idea."

' "I am very glad you did, and that you communicated it to me. I have now a key to all her odd looks and ways. Leave shame to her. If she does wrong, she ought to feel it."

' "She is not entirely without it, I think."

' "I do not see much sign of it. She is playing *Robin Adair* at this moment—*his* favourite." '[60]

Emma is being laughed at; she has never had a brother of her own age before, or she might realize what is happening.

When the ball is planned, it is to throw dust in the Westons' eyes that so much ado is made about consulting Miss Bates (in order that she may bring Jane).

Jane Fairfax seems to be aware of Emma's supposed complicity when she says: "Oh! Miss Woodhouse, I hope nothing may happen to prevent the ball. What a disappointment it would be! I do look forward to it, I own, with *very* great pleasure."[61]

Frank is summoned back to Enscombe, and the ball must be given up. He calls to bid Emma goodbye.

' "In short," said he, "perhaps, Miss Woodhouse—I think you can hardly be quite without suspicion—" '[62] Her only suspicion was that he meant to make her a declaration, and this (as she supposed) she warded off. He went away fairly sure that she knew his secret. Jane Fairfax was left suffering with headache to a degree, and was not seen again till she could show an 'odious' composure about the cancelled ball.

§5. The Intrigue (II)

In April, John Knightley brings little Henry and John to stay at Hartfield; his visit coincides with the dinner-party for the Eltons, to which Jane Fairfax is invited. John Knightley's conversation with Jane Fairfax reveals that she has been to the post-office, in the rain, and that it is her daily walk.

'Jane's solicitude about fetching her own letters had not escaped Emma. She had heard and seen it all; and felt some curiosity to know whether the wet walk of this morning had produced any. She suspected that it *had*; that it would not have been so resolutely encountered but in full expectation of hearing from someone very dear, and that it had not been in vain. She thought there was an air of greater happiness than usual—a glow both of complexion and spirits.'[63]

Mr Weston comes in after dinner; he brings a letter from Frank, announcing his speedy return. He goes round telling everyone; Jane Fairfax manages to be deep in conversation with John Knightley, and avoids a separate communication.

Frank returns, and Emma clearly perceives that he is not in love with her. 'Absence, with the conviction probably of her indifference, had produced this very natural and very desirable effect.'[64] But, all the same, 'He was not calm; his spirits were evidently fluttered; there was a restlessness about him.'

It was May, and the date of the ball was fixed. Emma went

early to the *Crown* on the evening. Frank showed 'a mind not at ease. He was looking about, he was going to the door, he was watching for the sound of other carriages'—afraid, Emma thought, of a return of his feeling for herself. He showed great impatience to meet Mrs Elton; it appears that she was to have brought Jane Fairfax and her aunt, but the carriage is sent back for them.

'In a few minutes the carriage returned.—Somebody talked of rain.—"I will see that there are umbrellas, sir," said Frank to his father: "Miss Bates must not be forgotten": and away he went.'[65]

Emma has forgotten, but the reader may remember that this is a charming family trait; so had Mr Weston first shown his interest in Miss Taylor. "Ever since the day (about four years ago) that Miss Taylor and I met with him in Broadway-lane, when, because it began to mizzle, he darted away with so much gallantry, and borrowed two umbrellas for us from Farmer Mitchell's, I made up my mind on the subject."[66]

There follows the scene when Emma taxes Frank with ingratitude to Mrs Elton; he is quite sure that she is in possession of his secret.

In June Mr Knightley's dislike of Frank Churchill increased, he 'began to suspect him of some inclination to trifle with Jane Fairfax . . . there were symptoms of intelligence between them. . . .'[67] He had first observed this at a dinner-party at the Elton's, at which Emma was not present.

Then came Frank Churchill's blunder; on an evening walk, he asked what became of Perry's plan of setting up his carriage. He believed that he had heard of it from Mrs Weston, but she denied all knowledge of it. He was therefore aware that he must know of it through his clandestine correspondence with Jane Fairfax, and tried to pass it off as something he must have dreamed.

' "Why, to own the truth," cried Miss Bates, who had been trying in vain to be heard the last two minutes, "if I must speak on this subject, there is no denying that Mr Frank Churchill might have—I do not mean to say that he did not dream it—I am sure I have sometimes the oddest dreams in the world—but if I am questioned about it, I must acknowledge that there was such an idea last spring; for Mrs Perry herself mentioned it to my mother, and the Coles knew of it as well as ourselves—but it was quite a secret, known to nobody else, and only thought of about three days. Mrs Perry was very anxious that he should have a carriage, and came to my mother in great spirits one morning because she thought she had prevailed. Jane, don't you remember grand-mama's telling us of it when we got home?—I forget where we had been walking to—very likely to Randalls; yes, I think it was to Randalls. Mrs Perry was always particularly fond of my mother— indeed I do not know who is not—and she had mentioned it to her in confidence; she had no objection to her telling us, of course, but it was not to go beyond: and, from that day to this, I never mentioned it to a soul that I know of. At the same time, I will not positively answer for my having never dropt a hint, because I do sometimes pop out a thing before I am aware. I am a talker, you know; I am rather a talker; and now and then I have let a thing escape me which I should not. I am not like Jane, I wish I were. I will answer for it *she* never betrayed the least thing in the world. Where is she?—Oh! just behind. Perfectly remember Mrs Perry's coming.—Extraordinary dream indeed!" '⁶⁸

With admirable skill, Jane Austen has given something like a messenger's speech to her bore. I will quote a former comment of my own. 'What a thing Miss Bates has now popped out! What a thing she has let escape her! In all her rambling speech, the essential points are not lost. The Perry's plan was known only to the Bates and the Coles—from "the worthy Coles" it would not get to Mr Frank Churchill. It was made known to Miss Bates and Jane Fairfax on their return from Mrs Weston's house—therefore the unlikelihood of their having dropt a hint to her is much increased. Miss Bates ends, with unconscious irony, by praising her niece's discretion, just as she has begun with unconscious irony: "if I must speak on this subject", when she had had to struggle for a hearing.'⁶⁹

They go into Hartfield and play the letter game. Frank gives Jane the word *blunder*, and Harriet publishes it. 'There was a blush on Jane's cheek which gave it a meaning not otherwise ostensible. Mr Knightley connected it with the dream; but how it could all be, was beyond his comprehension.'⁷⁰

Frank gives Emma the word *Dixon*, and then passes it to Jane, who is much displeased; she is (one supposes) tired of that joke, and thinks it no moment for joking. Frank anxiously pushes some more letters towards her, but she sweeps them away unexamined— we know (from family tradition) that the unread word was *pardon*.⁷¹

Mr Knightley now feels obliged to warn Emma that he has seen "symptoms of attachment"[72] between Frank and Jane, but she resolutely denies all possibility of such a thing.

Jane Fairfax is, by this time, in a state of great nervous irritability; the helplessness of the attachment, and the impossibility of its being concealed much longer are weighing on her spirits, and the Highbury household is trying her nerves to the utmost. Mrs Elton, also, is being a nuisance, with her well-meant job-hunting. Jane turns to Emma as a friend, and almost as an accomplice, to cover her flight from the strawberry-party at Donwell: "Miss Woodhouse, we all know at times what it is to be wearied in spirits. Mine, I confess, are exhausted. . . . Oh! Miss Woodhouse, the comfort of being sometimes alone!"[73]

Frank appeared late; he had met Jane on her way back to Highbury and wanted to walk with her, 'but she would not suffer it'.[74] They quarrelled. He arrived cross at Donwell.

Again Emma was almost made his confidante—it was also out of contrariness that he attached himself to her, because (as appears from his letter to Mrs Weston) Jane was vexed at his attentions to her, and he was thoroughly out of humour with Jane.

"I feel a strong persuasion, this morning, that I shall soon be abroad. I ought to travel", he tells her. And he complains: "I am thwarted in everything material. I do not consider myself at all a fortunate person."[75]

One remembers that at the Coles' dinner party, four months back, he told Emma that the wish to travel had left him.

Emma, who has never even seen the sea,[76] is not very sympathetic about travels in 'Swisserland'; perhaps she has something of the insularity of her creator, who wrote: 'I hope your letters from abroad are satisfactory. They would not be satisfactory to *me*, I confess, unless they breathed a strong spirit of regret for not being in England.'[77] That, after all, is not what people travel for.

The picnic on Box Hill is disastrous; the party is too large, the day is too hot. Frank Churchill and Emma 'flirted together excessively'; they were both depressed, and were aware that they were being silly, and rather vulgar.

' "Ladies and gentlemen," says Frank, "I am ordered by Miss Woodhouse (who, wherever she is, presides) to say that she desires to know what you are all thinking of." '

Mr Knightley's reply is crushing: "Is Miss Woodhouse sure that she would like to hear what we are all thinking of?"[78] Emma's snub to Miss Bates, a few minutes later, though less justified, is hardly a more cruel remark.

Frank further vents his ill-temper with Jane in this comment on the Eltons. "How well they suit one another!—Very lucky—marrying as they did, upon an acquaintance formed only in a public place!—They only knew each other, I think, a few weeks in Bath! Peculiarly lucky!—for as to any real knowledge of a person's disposition that Bath, or any public place, can give—it is all nothing; there can be no knowledge. It is only by seeing women in their own homes, among their own set, just as they always are, that you can form any just judgment. Short of that, it is all guess and luck—and will generally be ill-luck. How many a man has committed himself on a short acquaintance, and rued it all the rest of his life!"[79] Frank Churchill had met Jane Fairfax at Weymouth.

This lovers' quarrel has to be conducted decorously, and in public. Jane Fairfax is stopped in her reply by a cough, but then takes courage.

' "A hasty and imprudent attachment may arise—but there is generally time to recover from it afterwards. I would be understood to mean, that it can only be weak, irresolute characters (whose happiness must be always at the mercy of chance), who will suffer an unfortunate acquaintance to be an inconvenience, an oppression for ever." '[80]

This is tantamount to her dismissal of Frank Churchill; what Jane may think about Emma we are not precisely told, though her subsequent actions show that Emma is regarded as an enemy. Mr Knightley, at all events, fears that she has advanced far towards an engagement with Frank Churchill, for his reproach to her about her snub to Miss Bates is couched in the form of a last remonstrance: "Emma, I must once more speak to you as I have been used to do. . . ."[81]

That night, at the Eltons', Jane Fairfax decides to break with Frank Churchill, and to accept a post as a governess. She does so, when she hears that he has returned to Richmond, without seeking to be reconciled with her. It is Miss Bates who (unwittingly) gives us the sequence of events.

' "It was before tea—stay—no, it could not be before tea, because we were just going to cards—and yet it was before tea, because I remember thinking—Oh! no, now I recollect, now I have it; something happened before tea. . . . When Mr Elton came back, he told us what John Ostler had been telling him, and then it came out about the chaise having been sent to Randalls to take Mr Frank Churchill to Richmond. That was what happened before tea. It was after tea that Jane spoke to Mrs Elton."[82]

Thirty-six hours after Frank's return to Richmond, Mrs Churchill was dead.

§6. Mr Knightley

In all the four finished novels there is a basic resemblance in the plot—an outsider (or outsiders) come to a country place and upset the rhythm of life there. So different is the pattern, however, produced by each shake of the kaleidoscope, that there is little sameness about the books.

Emma has a further resemblance to *Mansfield Park* because it ends with a marriage between the heroine and her mentor.

This time, instead of the patient Fanny, we have a very wrongheaded heroine—one who (like Catherine Morland, Marianne Dashwood and Elizabeth Bennet) has to undergo a change of heart. But though we have a hero whose moral and intellectual superiority is most convincingly established, he also is in the dark about himself at the beginning of the book.

' "She always declares she will never marry, which, of course, means just nothing at all. But I have no idea that she has yet ever seen a man she cared for. It would not be a bad thing for her to be very much in love with a proper object. I should like to see Emma in love, and in some doubt of a return; it would do her good." '[84]

So he says (with wonderful dramatic irony) to Mrs Weston. Neither he, nor anyone else, is aware of the reason for his antecedent jealousy of Frank Churchill. (The reader is given a skilful misdirection here, in Emma's jealousy of Jane Fairfax;[85] this is not parallel, for it never has a sexual motive: Emma never seriously believes Mr Knightley to be attached to her.)

All through the book, Emma's particular tenderness about Mr Knightley's good opinion is obvious; when they quarrel (and this is most subtly done) they have lovers' quarrels with a brother-and-sister technique, inadequate to their needs. Dr Chapman[86] calls attention to occasions when Mr Knightley comes 'unbidden, and sometimes unrecognized into Emma's thoughts'. He is always her standard of what a man should be.

We are never so much in Mr Knightley's confidence as we are in Emma's; we cannot fix times and dates. 'He had been in love with Emma, and jealous of Frank Churchill, from about the same period, one sentiment having probably enlightened him as to the other. . . . The Box-Hill party had decided him on going away. He would save himself from witnessing again such permitted, encouraged attentions.'[87]

The slow and entirely convincing bringing-together of Emma and Mr Knightley might be the author's reply, if anyone objected (as Fanny Knight objected) to her failure with Edmund and Fanny in *Mansfield Park*; and we can believe in 'the perfect happiness of the union'.[88]

§7. Highbury

Emma is geographically nearer to Highbury than the Bennets were to Meryton, but socially not so near; there is no Aunt Phillips. She is, indeed, rather fussy about keeping apart from it. I do not know whether the author—who licenses some degree of conjecture, for she said:

> *I do not write for such dull elves*
> *As have not a great deal of ingenuity themselves*[89]

—would like us to conjecture that she is a little uncertain about her position, which rests on wealth and not land, and that when she is Mrs Knightley of Donwell Abbey she will feel more sure of herself.

Two propositions must be clearly stated (for some writers confuse them): Highbury is rather dull and second-rate, and Emma is quite right in thinking so; nevertheless, when she is petty, absurd or unkind through snobbery, Jane Austen does not wish us to admire her. It is not Emma, but Mr Knightley, who sets the moral standard in this book.

Sir Harold Nicolson, who has launched an attack on Jane Austen, more intended to be provocative than thoughtful, complains: 'The society which she depicts is mean and competitive, almost wholly uninterested in intellectual, spiritual or aesthetic values, and wastes time, energy and even passion upon the meaningless subtleties of social status.'[90] There is a good deal of truth in this, but it is no condemnation of the author, whose aim is to present interesting individuals and not an interesting world, and who is fully aware of the defects of the society among which her individuals move.

Here is the dinner-party at the 'worthy Coles' ': 'a few clever things said, a few downright silly, but by much the larger proportion neither the one nor the other—nothing worse than every day remarks, dull repetitions, old news, and heavy jokes'.[91]

This passage surely proves that Jane Austen was critical, and Emma quite rightly critical of Highbury. And if people lack intellectual, spiritual and aesthetic interests, it seems rather cruel to deprive them of 'the meaningless subtleties of social status' as a subject of conversation; they cannot always 'speak with exquisite calmness and gravity of the weather'.[92] It is indeed fortunate, for the sake of conversation in the English provinces, that there is so much variety in the weather and in social status that they need not (in the mouth of an amusing person) be uninteresting topics.

Sir Harold is much vexed with Emma for judging of Frank Churchill that 'his indifference to a confusion of rank, bordered too much on inelegance of mind'. He does not quote the next sentence: 'He could be no judge, however, of the evil he was holding cheap.'[93] Frank did not live in Highbury; he could afford to do a little promiscuous 'good mixing', and need know none of the people after the ball was over.

The caste system is a kindlier and more protective thing than many very sociable people can be aware of. If I am bored by the doctor's wife, it may be a consolation to me that I am below the notice of the duchess, and that the dentist's wife has no claim upon mine. Some people (I am aware) think the matter a very shocking subject for conversation; there seems to be a great human need to be shocked. I do not share it, myself; and if we are no longer allowed to be shocked by Lady Chatterley, that does not incline me to be shocked by Emma.

Sir Harold is so cross with her that he makes statements that cannot be substantiated from the text. That she was 'almost morbidly aware of the social differences between the second rate and the third rate of Highbury' is his conjecture (in spite of Harriet and Mr Elton); and one wonders why such awareness (if it existed) should be morbid. Awareness of nice distinctions between fauna and flora is not usually so stigmatized. A reference to the text[94] will at once expose his statement that the comparative newness of Mr Weston's family did him harm in her eyes—it did not, but it injured him with the Churchills, as it would. There is not the smallest justification for saying that 'Miss Austen disliked the yeomanry' because Emma in her wrong-headed (and quite sufficiently condemned and punished) match-making tried to detach Harriet Smith from Robert Martin. Her bossy interference with other people's lives was disagreeable, and the unkindness of the limited visit to Abbey Mill Farm that she imposed on Harriet was odious—and Emma herself felt some pain over it.[95] But it is not only snobbery that makes people do that sort of thing; I have known young people to do just as horrid things out of very unnecessary 'anger'. People whose behaviour to their neighbours is governed by social theory rather than by their better instincts, are not very likely to conduct themselves well, unless their theory is the Christian doctrine of Love, or the Bloomsbury doctrine of the sanctity of personal relations—these are not incompatible.

Sir Harold, of course, can only be playing with his readers when he complains that 'Emma denounced as "vulgar familiarity" Mrs Elton's reference to Mr Knightley as "Knightley" '. What else could Emma say of it? If a clergyman's wife, newly arrived in his neighbourhood, were to refer to him as 'Nicolson' when speaking to one of his oldest friends, I am sure he would think her a crass vulgarian, and I hope he would not be too squeamish to say so.

Emma's silliness is really open to attack when, for instance, she wants to teach a lesson to the 'worthy Coles' for presuming to ask her to dinner, or when she thinks that Mr Knightley does not make enough use of his carriage; but the author deals with her firmly in either case. The 'worthy Coles' hold back their invitation until she is very glad to receive it, and Mr Knightley calls her "Non-sensical girl!"[96]

Mr Knightley's reproof is spoken 'not at all in anger', and no one should be angry with Emma. Sir Harold Nicolson finds (he says) 'blatant cruelty' in 'so many' of Jane Austen's heroes and heroines—like most hostile critics, he refrains from quoting chapter and verse—he cannot in Emma, that generous creature, so swift to redress any small wrong she may have done, so open to correction. I think Sir Harold could not have had the novels very freshly in his mind when he wrote. Apart from Mrs Norris, what character is 'blatantly cruel'? And it is odd to call Mrs Norris a heroine.

There are people, I believe, who find Jane Austen antipathetic because she calls a spade a spade, and because she tells them some home-truths. "One should be sorry to see greater pride or refine-ment in the teacher of a school"[97]—as an academic person myself, I often ponder this text with profit, and I can think of people who would do well to hang it over their beds. And many a man 'so well understanding the gradations of rank below him' might be warned by Mr Elton's example against being 'so blind to what rose above'.[98]

*

The final answer to all complaints about the littleness of the world of Highbury is to be found in the beautiful passage where Emma looks on it from the door of Ford's shop. 'Much could not be hoped from the traffic of even the busiest part of Highbury;—Mr Perry walking hastily by, Mr William Cox letting himself in at the office door, Mr Cole's carriage horses returning from exer-cise, or a stray letter-boy on an obstinate mule, were the liveliest objects she could presume to expect; and when her eyes fell only on the butcher with his tray, a tidy old woman travelling home-wards from shop with her full basket, two curs quarrelling over a dirty bone and a string of dawdling children round the baker's little bow-window eyeing the ginger-bread, she knew that she had no reason to complain, and was amused enough; quite enough still to stand at the door. A mind lively and at ease, can do with seeing nothing, and can see nothing that does not answer.'[99]

There can have been fewer livelier minds than that of the author of *Emma*, and that mind was evidently at ease while she was writing this, her masterpiece, and could see nothing that did not answer.

§8. Personal Problems

Mrs Leavis writes: 'I believe we can in every novel see the writer exploring her own problems by dramatizing them, or in this way giving them relief.'[100] This may, with caution, be admitted. I do not, however, think (with Mrs Leavis) that the position of Emma in this book has anything to do with that of the motherless Fanny

Knight, mistress of Godmersham since the age of fifteen. Fanny, with her many brothers and sisters, and with maternal relations nearby at Goodnestone, was never so isolated as Emma; her father was not an invalid, and there is no reason to suppose that she was ever allowed to become so managing. She had not the importance of being an heiress, for her father had ten other children—indeed if his lawsuit over Chawton went the wrong way, she would be unlikely to have much of a fortune.

She has, in her exploration of her own heart (in which she was helped by a secret correspondence with her aunt) contributed to the story of Harriet.

Mr Plumtre, a suitor, had stayed at Godmersham. 'Your trying to excite your own feelings by a visit to his room amused me excessively.—The dirty Shaving Rag was exquisite!—Such a circumstance ought to be in print. Much too good to be lost.'[101] It is in print; the shaving rag has turned into a piece of court plaister and the stump of an old pencil.[102] Yet I cannot think that Fanny was divided, her situation being given to Emma, and her heart to Harriet—Emma's situation seems to me simply a promotion of Emma Watson into affluence (as Charlotte Brontë promoted her sister Emily into Shirley's position).

Nor am I able to agree that the creator of 'good Mr Woodhouse' enjoyed his foibles less than her readers do, or that we are intended to regard him as a nuisance; I do not think impatience with family invalids is here expressed. Emma managed to do what she really wanted (to marry Mr Knightley and to go to the sea-side) in spite of her father; there is no evidence of unfulfilled wishes on her part. Moreover, though Mrs Austen may possibly have had some valetudinarian habits, between the three of them (Cassandra and Jane Austen, and Martha Lloyd), she could easily be looked after, without being a restraint on anyone's liberty.

The personal problem touched in this book seems to me to be the predicament of single women, and their 'dreadful propensity for being poor'.

In her characteristic way, Jane Austen has divided the subject between two characters, aunt and niece: the dowerless girl, and the contented chatty spinster.

The lot of the future governess is always regarded with horror. 'With the fortitude of a devoted noviciate, she had resolved at one-and-twenty to complete the sacrifice, and retire from all the pleasures of life, of rational intercourse, equal society, peace and hope, to penance and mortification for ever.'[103] And thus Jane Fairfax always thinks of her chosen profession: "There are places in town, offices, where inquiry would soon produce something— Offices for the sale—not quite of human flesh—but of human intellect." Comparing the 'governess-trade' with the slave-trade, she says it is "widely different certainly as to the guilt of those who carry it on; but as to the greater misery of the victims, I do not know where it lies."[104]

One recollects a conversation between Emma and Elizabeth Watson. "Poverty is a great Evil, but to a woman of Education & feeling it ought not, it cannot be the greatest.—I would rather be Teacher at a School (and I can think of nothing worse) than marry a Man I did not like."—"I would rather do any thing than be Teacher at a school—said her sister. *I* have been at school, Emma, & know what a life they lead; *you* never have."[105]

There are sympathetic references in the Letters to governesses at Godmersham: Miss Allen ('hard at it, governing away—poor creature! I pity her though they *are* my nieces'[106]), and Anne Sharpe, whose friendship with Cassandra and Jane Austen seems to me one of the signs of their having been neglected by their sister-in-law, the mistress of the house.

Jane Austen, herself, was in no danger of 'governing'; though her mother was placed in reduced circumstances by her father's death, 'her income was raised to four hundred and sixty pounds a year by contributions of one hundred pounds from Edward, and fifty pounds from James, Henry and Frank respectively';[107] the last would have doubled his contribution had his mother allowed it. In looking at the lot of the governess, the author is perhaps indulging in some Lucretian contemplation of 'ills ourselves are exempt from', but only just exempt. There was no other way by which she could have supported herself.

She was always poor, and any little windfall like a gift from Edward, or Mrs Knight's 'fee' or (most welcome and surprising of all) payment for her work, was exceedingly welcome. But there is no indication that she was in real anxiety over money until, in her last illness, she felt a keen disappointment at the will of her uncle James Leigh Perrot. It was the last chance of her mother being made independent of her sons. They were generous sons and brothers, but two of them (James and Frank) were married men.

Jane Austen was near enough to Miss Bates's predicament to feel it. "She is poor; she has sunk from the comforts she was born to; and, if she live to old age, must probably sink more."[108] So says Mr Knightley. The author's introduction to this character tells us that she 'stood in the very worst predicament in the world for having much of the public favour; and she had no intellectual superiority to make atonement to herself, or to frighten those who might hate her, into outward respect'.[109] The last words are surprisingly strong; there is hardly anything like them in all Jane Austen's novels. It is impossible not to feel that here she is very near to the bone.

She, of course, had the intellectual superiority to make atonement to herself, or to frighten those who might hate her into outward respect. I am not distressed at the thought that she may sometimes have used this superiority. I am only grieved for her if she needed to use it. She would not have used it without a cause; the good-hearted, the well-mannered, the simple would have had nothing to fear from her. If she did execution upon the Eltons of her world, who can blame her?

But, unlike Miss Bates, who was a 'talker', it seems that she scared by silence those whom she did not like. Mary Russell Mitford wrote: 'A friend of mine who visits her now, says that she has stiffened into the most perpendicular, precise, taciturn piece of "single blessedness" that ever existed, and that, till *Pride and Prejudice* showed what a precious gem was hidden in that unbending case, she was no more regarded in society than a poker or a fire-screen, or any other thin, upright piece of wood or iron that fills the corner in peace and quietness. The case is very different now: she is still a poker—but a poker of whom every one is afraid.'[110] But Miss Mitford owns that her friend, though 'truth itself', was a sister-in-law of that Mr Baverstock who laid claim against Edward Knight to the Chawton property. Jane Austen was too strong a partisan of her brother's rights to have unbent in such company, and the generalization 'every one is afraid' (sufficiently belied by other evidence) is as worthless as such generalizations usually are.

In so achieved a masterpiece as this, personal problems are very completely sublimated. I remember a distinguished lecturer on

Greek drama pointing out that in its irony and its skilful anag-
norisis (or 'recognition') and peripeteia this novel is, in its own way,
as triumphantly successful as the *Oedipus Rex*, Aristotle's ideal tragedy. Such works do not tell one much about their authors.

Persuasion

§1. Its History

Persuasion was published with *Northanger Abbey* after the author's death, in 1818. Henry Austen was, presumably, responsible for both titles. It had been begun 'before she went to London in the autumn of 1815 for the publication of *Emma*',[1] and she wrote 'Finis' at the end of the first draft on 18 July 1816,[2] exactly twelve months before she died. Having felt dissatisfied with the tenth chapter of the second volume, which was to have been the penultimate chapter of the novel, she rewrote it in August 1816, as the existing tenth and eleventh chapters—the manuscript of the cancelled chapter has survived.

On 13 March 1817 she wrote to Fanny Knight: 'I have a something ready for Publication, which may perhaps appear about a twelvemonth hence. It is short, about the length of Catherine.'[3] Ten days later, she added: 'You will not like it, so you need not be impatient. You may *perhaps* like the Heroine, as she is almost too good for me.'[4] The authors of the *Life* believe that the delay in publishing 'shows how unwilling she was to let anything go till she was quite sure she had polished it to the utmost', and imagine that the story of Mrs Smith would have been brought to life 'by touches which she knew so well how to impart', had her health been restored.[5] In short, they encourage us to give a liberal interpretation to the words 'ready for Publication', and to believe that a great deal more work was to have been done on it.

Mrs Leavis, who calls this work *The Elliots*, writes: 'The prototype, which exists for every other novel, could hardly have not existed for this work, and as the author's hands were full from 1806 onwards, it can possibly be allotted to the pre-1806 gap.'[6]

There is no necessity for a 'prototype'; Jane Austen was surely capable of doing something entirely new. This is demonstrated by *Sanditon*, which has all the air of a 'prototype'. (*Sanditon* is, indeed, too prototypal to be of great interest; the chief value to us of its survival is that it corrects misapprehensions about *Persuasion*. The melancholy of *Persuasion* can hardly be due to ill health, when in worse health the author wrote those almost farcical chapters. *Persuasion* is melancholy because Jane Austen intended it.)

A 'prototype' need not be assumed, the more so that *Persuasion* can hardly be regarded as a finished work. Such a thing, however, may have existed; it would not be strange if the Bath years had produced a second Bath story.

The beautiful autumnal quality of the love story must be of recent inspiration. Virginia Woolf was certainly right in saying that the great conversation between Anne and Captain Harville 'proves not merely the biographical fact that Jane Austen had loved, but the aesthetic fact that she was no longer afraid to say so. Experience, when it was of a serious kind, had to sink very deep, and to be thoroughly disinfected by the passage of time, before she allowed herself to deal with it in fiction.'[7]

I think it is from Miss Lascelles that we can get a hint as to the original character of *The Elliots* (supposing such an early work to have existed). She rightly indicates a second theme in the novel as we have it: 'the bursting open, for Anne, of the prison that Sir Walter and Elizabeth have made of Kellynch—the expansion of her world'.[8] The Cinderella theme had always been a favourite with Jane Austen; and there are other subjects in this book that might have been written up from early sketches, such as the happy, unintellectual Musgrove family, and the naval world of the Harvilles and the Crofts. All such things might lie about in the author's mind or in her notebooks, until she discovered the history of Anne Elliot; and then the Spirit blew, and they were created.

§2. Mrs Smith

No part of the novel has caused greater dissatisfaction than the story of Mrs Smith.

The function of Mrs Smith is to apprise Anne of the bad character of Mr Elliot. She is intended to be a good character, to give authority to her evidence; at the end of the book she and Lady Russell are the 'two friends in the world'[9] that Anne (forgetting the Musgroves) has to contribute to the common stock, when she marries Captain Wentworth.

Mrs Smith, of course, is brave in adversity; she has 'that elasticity of mind, that disposition to be comforted, that power of turning readily from evil to good, and of finding employment which carried her out of herself, which was from Nature alone'.[10]

Hideous as the work of her hands probably is—'little thread-cases, pin-cushions and card-racks'—it is an amusement in her sad life, confined to a noisy parlour and a dark back-bedroom, and it helps her to do some good to the poor.

Nor can she be blamed for her pleasure in gossip, at which Anne does not cavil. But the pleasure is carried rather too far; there is in it not only the vulgarity of listening to servants' talk, but an element of espionage and treachery. Worst of all, Mrs Smith sits gloating in the middle of the web that she has spun; her tone is so very unpleasant that even Anne protests. "It does not come to me in quite so direct a line as that; it takes a bend or two, but nothing of consequence. The stream is as good as at first; the little rubbish it collects in the turnings, is easily moved away."[11] Here, perhaps, only Mrs Smith's tone is at fault, and a few verbal corrections might put it right.

Very much worse is her commendation of Mr Elliot. "Let me plead for my—present friend I cannot call him—but for my former friend. Where can you look for a more suitable match? Where could you expect a more gentlemanlike, agreeable man? Let me recommend Mr Elliot. I am sure you hear nothing but good of him from Colonel Wallis; and who can know him better than Colonel Wallis?"[12]

This is not very pleasant irony; Mrs Smith thinks she knows Mr Elliot a good deal better than Colonel Wallis can. When she is satisfied that Anne's affections are engaged elsewhere, she bursts into a tirade against him, ending: "Oh! he is black at heart, hollow and black!"[13]

There follows her account of his relations with her husband and herself. 'Anne could not but express some surprise at Mrs Smith's having spoken of him so favourably in the beginning of their conversation. "She had seemed to recommend and praise him!"'[14]

Mrs Smith's excuse is quite inadequate: "there was nothing else to be done". She had believed that Anne was certainly going to marry Mr Elliot. "I could no more speak the truth of him, than if he had been your husband. My heart bled for you, as I talked of happiness." If Mrs Smith had been a good friend and an honest woman, she might at least have held her tongue.

As things are, one feels an extreme distaste for Mrs Smith, and for her confederate Nurse Rooke—so 'delighted to be in the way'[15] to let Anne in, so curious to see her, that we imagine her on the watch for Lady Russell's carriage, that handsome equipage, well known to convey a Miss Elliot.[16]

Unsatisfactory as the character of Mrs Smith is, it is yet more acceptable than her story. The main charge against Mr Elliot is that he led Mr Smith into ruin, by 'prompting and encouraging expenses'[17] that were beyond his means. As Mr Smith was at least his own age, and seems likely even to have been his senior, it can only have been his own fault (and that of his wife) if he let himself be so led; there is no suggestion that Mr Elliot made anything out of it.

Mrs Smith was "an injured, angry woman";[18] she 'did not want to take blame to herself, and was most tender of throwing any on her husband'.[19] In short, hers was the sort of story that momentarily carries conviction because of the passion with which it is narrated, but that will not bear investigation in a cool hour. Anne would have found it rather difficult to relate to Lady Russell, and Lady Russell might well have thought that no sufficient argument had been adduced against the eligible marriage between Anne and her father's heir.

The second part of the indictment is certainly worse: Mr Elliot had been selfish and negligent, had refused to act as Charles Smith's executor, and had treated his widow with 'cold civility' and 'hard-hearted indifference'. 'It was a dreadful picture of ingratitude and inhumanity'[20]—but we cannot so easily forget that earlier the same morning Mrs Smith had spoken of the trouble she wished Mr Elliot to take as something "which it is very natural for him now, with so many affairs and engagements of his own, to avoid and get rid of as he can—very natural, perhaps. Ninety-nine out of a hundred would do the same."[21]

Mrs Smith's affairs in the West Indies are not at all well worked out; 'a little trouble in the right place'[22] might recover her property. This was proved to be the case, because Captain Wentworth ultimately put her in the way of recovering it 'by writing for her, acting for her, and seeing her through all the petty difficulties of the case, with the activity and exertion of a fearless man [What was there to fear?] and a determined friend'.[23] The fact that Captain Wentworth was able to do this, proves that Mr Elliot's assistance, as executor, was not essential. It is hard to believe that

Mrs Smith, with her 'elasticity of mind' was incapable of writing business letters. Her 'bodily weakness'[24] would hardly have been an impediment, as it did not prevent her from knitting; and though 'she could not afford to purchase the assistance of the law', an enterprising attorney could surely have been found to take up so promising a case as a speculation.

The whole story of Mrs Smith, mainly related as it is in the form of summary, is surely no more than a rough outline; Jane Austen could not have been satisfied with it as it was, and must have meant to go back to it to give it consistency and life.

§3. Mr Elliot

Mr Elliot's function in the plot is to make Captain Wentworth jealous. But, first, he performs the important service of revealing to him that Anne is still attractive. When he was still a stranger to them, at Lyme, 'he looked at her with a degree of earnest admiration, which she could not be insensible of. . . . Captain Wentworth looked round at her instantly in a way which showed his noticing of it. He gave her a momentary glance,—a glance of brightness, which seemed to say, "That man is struck with you,—and even I, at this moment, see something like Anne Elliot again."[25] It is the turning-point in the story.

On this first appearance, it was enough that he should be a gentleman, and well enough looking; when he reappears in Bath as the acknowledged cousin and as Anne's suitor, more is required. He must be thoughtful and sensible, and with some charm of manner. Marriage between them must seem plausible as well as eligible.

But Jane Austen, who has so far (for we must not speak of this book as a finished work) been unsuccessful in establishing Mrs Smith's credit, has done rather too much for Mr Elliot's; like Lady Russell, we must suffer 'some pain in understanding and relinquishing'[26] him. Other people can appreciate Anne's beauty of character and person; no one, so much as Mr Elliot, seems to realize the beauty of her mind. He shows so much of the highest kind of taste, that we cannot easily believe him to be "without heart or conscience".[27]

After a month's acquaintance with Mr Elliot, Anne felt an increasing mistrust of him—but her reasons for this are contradictory: on the one hand, he was too cautious, too reserved; on the other: 'The names which occasionally dropt of former associates, the allusions to former practices and pursuits, suggested suspicions not favourable of what he had been. She saw that there had been bad habits; that Sunday travelling had been a common thing. . . .'[28] This lamentable passage, with a few verbal changes, could be made much more acceptable. Mr Elliot, it would be explained, now professed correct opinions (including religious orthodoxy)—at one time he must have been, at least, careless of his religious duties (as was proved by his frequent travelling on Sundays). If we regard such passages as the author's notes, and not as the final text, we shall judge them more fairly. We may also remember that to many of a gentleman's worse habits Anne could hardly refer, even in her own mind.

But the question may be asked, could Jane Austen ever have made a satisfactory thing of the character of Mr Elliot? Not altogether, I am afraid, for it must need some comprehension of a smart and rather raffish London life, and she had failed in just this when creating Henry and Mary Crawford.

The documentary evidence against Mr Elliot is of the flimsiest; it is a letter written more than eleven years ago, and when he was only twenty-three. He then spoke most disrespectfully of the Kellynch family, and it was not at all unnatural that he should. He meant to marry money, and the Elliots' scheme of marrying him to Elizabeth could have no appeal for him. As a poor man (with his temper tried by Sir Walter) it was most natural that he should speak with impatience of his reversion of the baronetcy which could only be a burden to him. When he had become rich, it was equally natural that he should think differently. The production of this letter (now eleven years old) does nothing, apart from establishing the vindictiveness of Mrs Smith.

The diamond-cut-diamond intrigue of Mr Elliot and Mrs Clay is only roughly sketched in. The two insinuating creatures matched against each other, and finally pairing off, are well enough set in the background of a watering-place during the season. The situation probably derives, through eighteenth-century literature, from Restoration drama. It is not, however, a situation with which Jane Austen was well equipped to deal—'Let other pens dwell on guilt and misery.'

§4. Lady Russell

Lady Russell is a 'sensible, deserving woman';[29] she thinks of herself as 'steady and matter of fact,'[30] and is conventional both in her ideas and in her appearance—"Something so formal and *arrangé* in her air! and she sits so upright!"[31] She is, perhaps, more intellectual than intelligent; she "quite bores one with her new publications" ("all the new poems and states of the nation that come out"). It is not surprising that she has never listened to Anne's music with 'any just appreciation or real taste'[32]—Captain Wentworth was the only person to do that, since Lady Elliot died. 'There is a quickness of perception in some, a nicety in the discernment of character, a natural penetration, in short, which no experience in others can equal'[33]—Lady Russell was not much 'gifted in this part of understanding'.

'But she was a very good woman, and if her second object was to be sensible and well-judging, her first was to see Anne happy. She loved Anne better than she loved her own abilities'—this is (like Mr Elliot's) 'praise, warm, just, and discriminating, of Lady Russell'.[34]

There is a touch of humour in her cosy complacency: "I hope I shall remember, in future, . . . not to call at Uppercross in the Christmas holidays."[35] And it is with an amused affection that we see her spirits rise on entering Bath, 'amidst the dash of carriages, the heavy rumble of carts and drays, the bawling of newsmen, and the ceaseless clink of pattens'. We allow her her own choice of 'winter pleasures'—card-parties, if she prefers them to the company of noisy children—though she is too apt to think that Bath must suit everybody, because she herself is so fond of it.

Once, only, the author 'goes behind' her, and our one glimpse of her mind is not amiable; 'internally her heart revelled in angry pleasure, in pleased contempt'[36] that Captain Wentworth, who had once appreciated Anne, should now show his inferiority by appearing to be in love with Louisa Musgrove. But she does not know that Anne is suffering, and she may be allowed some anger on her protégée's behalf, and some satisfaction in being right. And there is one person who would never blame her, if he could know of her contempt—Captain Wentworth himself.

This excellent, limited woman, 'rather of sound than of quick

abilities',[37] plays the role of Peitho, the goddess of Persuasion.
Perhaps she is not very well cast.

When Henry Austen gave this book the title *Persuasion* (and he
may, for all we know, have been following the author's wish) he
added immensely to the connotation of the word; we can hardly
hear it now without thinking of the whole exquisite novel, of the
shore of Lyme, the streets of Bath, and the autumnal hedgerows of
Uppercross. It has become one of the most beautiful words in the
language, but that is not what Jane Austen intended. Anne had,
she decided in the end, been right to yield to the persuasion of an
older friend, though that friend had been mistaken in the advice
she gave. Persuasion means over-persuasion.

There are several indications that Lady Russell was to have been
built up into a generally more persuasive person. "If we can persuade your father to all this",[38] are her first words, as she looks
over Anne's plan for retrenchment; but we very soon learn that
she 'had scarcely any influence with Elizabeth . . . had never succeeded in any point which she wanted to carry, against previous
inclination'.[39] At Uppercross, the simple uncultivated Musgroves
seem to regard her as a monster of culture and persuasion—and
yet they knew nothing of the early history of Anne and Captain
Wentworth.

Louisa, telling Captain Wentworth that Anne had not accepted
her brother's proposal, said: "pappa and mamma always think it
was her great friend Lady Russell's doing, that she did not.—They
think Charles might not be learned and bookish enough to please
Lady Russell, and that therefore, she persuaded Anne to refuse
him."[40] (In fact 'Lady Russell had lamented her refusal'.[41])

At Lyme, Anne goes for an early walk with Henrietta, and enters
most sympathetically into her plans. Dr Shirley, the rector of
Uppercross, ought to settle in Lyme for the benefit of the sea air.
An active, respectable young man (Charles Hayter) ought to be
established in Uppercross as a resident curate; and it would be an
advantage if the curate were married.

' "I wish," said Henrietta, very well pleased with her companion,
"I wish Lady Russell lived at Uppercross, and were intimate with
Dr Shirley. I have always heard of Lady Russell, as a woman of
the greatest influence with every body! I always look upon her as
able to persuade a person to anything! I am afraid of her, as I
have told you before, quite afraid of her, because she is so **very**

clever; but I respect her amazingly, and wish we had such a neighbour at Uppercross." '

'Anne was amused by Henrietta's manner of being grateful, and amused also, that the course of events and the new interests of Henrietta's mind should have placed her friend at all in favour with any of the Musgrove family. . . .'[42] And yet, but for her over-hearing in the hedgerow, the reader is given no evidence that Lady Russell is unpopular at Uppercross.

Like Mrs Smith and Mr Elliot, other characters functional in Anne's story, Lady Russell has not been completely worked out. The inadequacy of these key characters (as well as the nature of Anne's story) persuades me that they belong to an upper stratum of the author's work; the Crofts and Musgroves (I believe) come from deeper down. When Mrs Woolf found a 'flatness' in much of *Persuasion*, I think she may have meant much the same thing. I question her explanation of it, that the author was in a transitional stage in her work—it might or might not be true (and to our lasting sorrow we shall never know what she would have done next. *Sanditon* is too vestigial to afford any true criterion). I think that Jane Austen had drawn so much out of her stock-pot in recent years, that she was having to put in new ingredients; time, alas, was not allowed her for them to simmer to mellowness.

§5. Irony

Miss Lascelles admirably points out that irony 'is the very tongue in which *Persuasion* is written'.[43] Against the true and deep feeling of Anne, of Captain Harville and of Captain Wentworth, false and shallow (though not unamiable) feeling is exposed for what it is. This approach to her subject guarded her from the danger of sentimentality, and the critic who follows it will be able to defend her against two objections to the book that are commonly made.

The first arises out of the episode of "poor Richard". The first mention of Captain Wentworth's name recalls 'thick-headed, un-feeling, unprofitable Dick Musgrove' to his family's recollection, for he had been six months in Captain Wentworth's frigate, the *Laconia*.

'The real circumstances of this pathetic piece of family history were, that the Musgroves had had the ill fortune of a very trouble-some, hopeless son, and the good fortune to lose him before he reached his twentieth year; that he had been sent to sea, because he was stupid and unmanageable on shore; that he had been very little cared for at any time by his family, though quite as much as he deserved; seldom heard of, and scarcely at all regretted, when the intelligence of his death abroad had worked its way to Upper-cross, two years before.'[44]

A sad little story, but without the dignity of tragedy. I think some sentimental readers are unwilling to believe that Dick Mus-grove was quite 'hopeless'; but any boy at school (and any man who accurately remembers his school-days) knows how surprisingly, dreadfully young, the character of the sullen, incorrigible oaf reveals itself. Jane Austen probably knew such creatures among the sons of country neighbours, and had, no doubt, heard from her brothers, Frank and Charles, about 'such midshipmen as every captain wishes to get rid of'. Captain Wentworth, Charles Mus-grove and Anne, in their different ways, may be trusted for their reading of the story.

The revived thought of Dick, and the reperusal of his letters by his mother, 'her poor son gone for ever, and all the strength of his faults forgotten, had affected her spirits exceedingly, and thrown her into greater grief for him than she had known on first hearing of his death'. It was a cosy grief, to be soothed by the harp, and talk, and cheerful company.

The unreal and rather pleasing quality of this grief is further manifested when Captain Wentworth dines at Uppercross: "Ah! Miss Anne, if it had pleased Heaven to spare my poor son, I dare say he would have been just such another by this time."[45]

This is, of course, ridiculous. Miss Lascelles excellently com-ments: 'So long as grief lived, she would surely be apt to forget the graceless boy in the child endearingly dependent on her forbear-ance. Now she dallies instead with the fiction of a brilliant future forestalled by death. . . .'[46] Jane Austen knew how a mother really grieves for a child; she particularly admired the part of Constance in *King John*.[47]

Captain Wentworth, a tender-hearted man 'shewed the kindest consideration of all that was real and unabsurd in the parent's feelings'.[48] What follows, has proved a stumbling-block to many: 'Captain Wentworth should be allowed some credit for the self-command with which he attended to her large fat sighings over the destiny of a son, whom alive nobody had cared for.'

Many people are (or profess themselves to be) even more shocked by the following paragraph; they think that Jane Austen, not content with being callous and tasteless, has rubbed it in.

'Personal size and mental sorrow have certainly no necessary proportions. A large bulky figure has as good a right to be in deep affliction, as the most graceful set of limbs in the world. But, fair or not fair, there are unbecoming conjunctions, which reason will patronize in vain,—which taste cannot tolerate,—which ridicule will seize.'

Miss Elizabeth Jenkins, in her most sympathetic book, [49] calls this comment 'inadmissible', and is convinced that it would have come out in revision.

It might; but first of all, we must admit that it is perfectly true. The stage sorrow of obese opera-singers is a perennial joke. Moreover (as Miss Jenkins is fully aware), a person as sensitive as Jane Austen may be impatient of affected feeling, and is far more likely to make a ruthless remark than many people with thicker skins, and she would stand by her ruthless remarks. I once knew a very cruel woman who used to sigh over the premature deaths of total strangers as reported in *The Times*. Such a one would not have made the pleasing jest about Mrs Hall of Sherborne's baby.

But it is Miss Lascelles who has put us on the right track; we are shortly going to see a far more personable character indulging in pleasing sorrow. We are to be prepared for this spectacle; many readers are not, and begin by taking Captain Benwick as seriously as he takes himself. If he had weighed four or five stone more, no one would fall into such an error.

'He has a pleasing face and a melancholy air, just as he ought to have.' [50] The history of his private life 'rendered him perfectly interesting in the eyes of all the ladies'; [51] he had been engaged to Captain Harville's sister, who had died during the summer, and the mourning of her loss was now his full-time occupation. Everyone and everything had combined to indulge and cosset his grief. Captain Wentworth had gone (without leave) to break the news to him, and had not left him for a week. Since then he had been on shore, living with the Harville family, who generously deferred to his grief as greater than their own. And his 'tolerable collection of well-bound volumes' [52] (being, in all probability, mainly composed of romantic poetry) was food for his sorrow.

Anne, from the first, was not entirely taken in: "he has not, perhaps, a more sorrowing heart than I have. I cannot believe his prospects so blighted for ever. He is younger than I am; younger in feeling, if not in fact; younger as a man. He will rally again, and be happy with another."[53] A neat turn of the plot will render both Anne and Captain Benwick happy; he is, as it were, the ram in the thicket, whose sacrifice to Louisa Musgrove will set Captain Wentworth free.

Anne had a literary conversation with him, the one indulgence that the Harvilles were unable to give him. 'Though shy, he did not seem reserved'—[54] he was a shallow, emotional person. It can be seen at once that Jane Austen is amusing herself, when Benwick and Anne discuss 'how ranked the *Giaour* and *The Bride of Abydos*; and moreover, how the *Giaour* was to be pronounced'. By the end of the chapter, he has completely given himself away: 'he repeated, with such tremulous feeling, the various lines which imaged a broken heart, or a mind destroyed by wretchedness, and looked so entirely as if he meant to be understood'. When Anne checked him, telling him of the danger of poetry to strong feelings, he looked 'not pained, but pleased with this allusion to his situation'.[55] For three months he had been *le ténébreux, le veuf, l'inconsolé* —a fine role. Now the part was almost pure enjoyment to him. Anne had grieved in silence for eight years, and the last thing she had wanted was to be understood.

It is all very well for Captain Benwick to rally (and a very great relief to the principals in this novel), nevertheless it is 'too soon', and also too complete. "A man like him, in his situation! With a heart pierced, wounded, almost broken! Fanny Harville was a very superior creature; and his attachment to her was indeed attachment. A man does not recover from such a devotion of the heart to such a woman!—He ought not—he does not."[56] He might, after several years, marry a Louisa Musgrove, as a sort of make-shift second marriage, and without too much romance about it. He should not (within nine months of Fanny's death) be sitting at Louisa's elbow "reading verses, or whispering to her, all day long."[57] He has loved and lost love, which is replaceable, not an irreplaceable person.

The scene on the Cobb (against which many objections have been made) is far more acceptable when it is seen as part of this ironic pattern. It is not (as some people have thought) failed tragedy. It is a particularly difficult kind of scene to write, for there must be some suspension, not of disbelief, but of belief. Louisa's fall and concussion must be alarming, and yet the reader must not be too much harrowed, or he will expect her to die, and will feel cheated if she does not. (The accident-prone characters of Charlotte Yonge never disappoint people in this way.) Shakespeare shows himself aware of this kind of difficulty in the scene of Juliet's mock funeral. If the grief were real, we should be revolted at the callousness of Friar Laurence's plan. The Capulets and Paris are therefore not allowed to mourn sincerely over the living corpse, but indulge in the most frigid euphuisms, and old Capulet shows a touch of nature in his regret for the spoilt party. The Nurse is given a real wail, but it comes from the servants' hall rather than the heart. Shakespeare and Jane Austen are being tactful, and perhaps we do not like tact being used on us obtrusively in life or in letters. Probably scenes that require it should not be written.

Louisa insists on being jumped down the steps of the Cobb by Captain Wentworth: 'she was too precipitate by half a second, she fell on the Lower Cobb, and was taken up lifeless!'[58]

The accident might be more plausibly contrived, and Miss Lascelles has put forward the brilliant conjecture that Louisa was meant to be thrown out of a gig, as Mrs Croft so frequently was.[59]

"If I loved a man, as she loves the Admiral, I would always be with him, nothing should separate us, and I would rather be overturned by him, than driven safely by anybody else";[60] so Louisa had spoken, on the walk to Winthrop. And it would have been easy enough to overturn her.

But Miss Lascelles thinks that Jane Austen was deflected from her purpose by remembering the deaths of her friend, Mrs Lefroy, and her cousin, Jane Williams, in road accidents. This may very well be so, and in revision she might have found greater courage.

The episode is a little flat, but it is not absurd, and Sir Herbert Read need not have picked from it phrases 'which are not congruous with the tragedy of the situation',[61] for it is not tragic; and he should not (I think) have compared it with a tragic moment in *Wuthering Heights*, for there are no grounds for the comparison.

It is, as Miss Lascelles describes it, a 'counterfeit catastrophe'; and, as she observes, after the immediate reactions of the party, the fainting of Henrietta, the hysterics of Mary, and the self-command of Anne and Captain Wentworth, 'a familiar voice penetrates the babble of the poor Musgroves, a voice which no one who has heard it before can fail to recognize for Jane Austen's own':[62]

'By this time the report of the accident had spread among the workmen and boatmen about the Cobb, and many were collected near them, to be useful if wanted, at any rate, to enjoy the sight of a dead young lady, nay, two dead young ladies, for it proved twice as fine as the first report.'[63]

By this time, no discerning reader can be in any anxiety for Louisa.

§6. The Voice of True Feeling

Captain Benwick and the Musgroves are people who claim our sympathy, and it is no heavy irony that has been directed against them. Their feelings are perfectly amiable, though not quite what they think them to be. If they were hypocrites they would form too coarse a contrast to the delicate feelings of those two saints of the affections, Anne and Captain Harville.

Captain Wentworth is their equal in sensibility; but for the first part of the book he is sinning against the light, and acting against his peace. Pride has set him on, and very nearly loses him his happiness; had he been less proud, he and Anne might have come together again six years before.[64] It was 'angry pride'[65] that had made him try to attach himself to Louisa. The 'counterfeit catastrophe' showed him that he cared nothing for her, that he cared for Anne as deeply as ever, and that he was so dangerously entangled with Louisa, that he might have to marry her. If Henry James had been his creator, he would have fared badly indeed; strange American notions of chivalry would have forced him to press his suit with Louisa, just because he was so anxious not to succeed. He and Anne would have been allowed a moment's piercing revelation of their love—probably on a staircase—and then she and Henrietta would have attended Louisa when Dr Shirley married her to Captain Wentworth in Uppercross church. Luckily his sense of honour, though nice, was not high falutin: 'He would gladly weaken, by any fair means, whatever feelings or speculations concerning him might exist.'[66] He went into Shropshire, and the glad news of his release followed him.

Jane Austen said that Anne Elliot (who is, indeed, faultless to a degree that, before reading this book, one might have thought unattainable without dullness) was 'almost too good' for her. An otherwise unknown Mrs Barrett has said: 'Anne Elliot was herself; her enthusiasm for the navy and her perfect unselfishness, reflect her completely.'[67] But it was the same Mrs Barrett who has told us that Jane Austen never put living people into books: 'She said that she thought it quite fair to note peculiarities and weaknesses, but that it was her desire to create, not to reproduce; "besides", she added, "I am too proud of my gentlemen to admit that they were only Mr A. or Colonel B." '[68]

If she noted 'peculiarities and weaknesses', we may conjecture that she made some use of them; if (and few novelists do) she did not put people into books, yet (as every novelist does) she used people in them; and though her gentlemen were certainly not *only* Mr A. or Colonel B., it is likely that Mr A. and Colonel B. entered into their composition. She may (and more than she knew) have contributed to the character of Anne Elliot.

Miss Jenkins very well points out that Jane Austen was a much livelier person than Anne, who could not conceivably have written *Pride and Prejudice* or *Emma*; she also observes that Jane Austen's disappointment in love, and her fortitude in concealing it, have set their mark on the story. Then (as I think) she goes a little astray: 'whereas Anne could never have loved again, Jane Austen in her own person boldly rebutted the idea that one could be blighted for life by such an incident. As she said to Fanny Knight: "It is no creed of mine, as you must be well aware, that such sort of disappointments kill anybody." She said of Anne Elliot that the "only natural, happy and sufficient cure", a second attachment, had not been possible to her, because the limited society in which she moved did not provide anybody whom she could love. The author therefore was prepared to believe that circumstances made a second attachment impossible to Anne Elliot; but Anne herself did not believe that her actual marriage with Captain Wentworth would have cut her off from other men more decidedly than her own feelings for him. . . .'[69] I regretfully feel obliged to pick a number of holes in this passage.

First of all, we must place the remark to Fanny Knight in its proper context; Jane Austen[70] is urging her niece to give up Mr Plumtre if she cannot love him, and she very naturally insists that he will not die of the disappointment. Men do not die of love, and this is one of the things that *Persuasion* teaches us. But one might resist dying of love, and yet not love again; the first is a duty, the second is not.

Secondly, I cannot admit that what Anne 'believes' has any value as evidence in the face of what her creator said about her. And at the beginning of the book, before the reappearance of Captain Wentworth, we are told that 'time had softened down much, perhaps nearly all of peculiar attachment to him'.[71] But he had set a high standard, and Charles Musgrove was not good enough for her, as Harris Bigg-Wither was not good enough for Jane Austen—and as Louisa Musgrove should not have been good enough for James Benwick.

Lastly, Anne's story is different from Jane Austen's, for Captain Wentworth was alive, and returned into her life. It may (in a way) be a wish-fulfilment story, as *Pride and Prejudice* may have fulfilled earlier wishes. Now that 'time had softened down much, perhaps nearly all of peculiar attachment' Jane Austen felt able to write it. The epigraph might be (had it then been written) *Oh, that 'twere possible, after long grief and pain. . . .*

Death makes a difference. If Captain Wentworth had died, the memory of him would inevitably be dimmed and stylized. A few months' courtship—an essentially forward-looking relation—could scarcely produce the 'living love' with which Cassandra spoke of her sister till her own life's end; such a thing comes from years of shared life looked back on.

If he had suffered worse than death (that is, marriage to Louisa) Anne would have been quite as dutiful as Fanny Price, and would have made every effort to banish 'his idea'. But from very soon after they met again at Uppercross, she had new words or acts of kindness to cherish, even if conscious hope were not yet present. Moreover, Anne was pleased with Mr Elliot's admiration at Lyme, was even sexually interested (she 'felt that she should like to know who he was'[72]); and she was not so much resigned to loss of bloom but that (encouraged by Mr Elliot's looks and Lady Russell's compliments) she had the amusement 'of hoping that she was to be blessed with a second spring of youth and beauty'.[73] Her life as a woman was not yet over, even when hope was at its lowest.

In short, though we must not say that Anne Elliot *is* Jane Austen, (and in some respects she is unlike her), their attitude to love and much of their experience is identical.

Each had loved and had lost, and had courageously hidden her grief; each was left with an ideal, though she had recovered from most of the 'peculiar attachment'; each was naturally fastidious (and the more so, from once having seen a man whom she could love); each lived in too narrow a circle to be likely to form a second attachment; each rejected the proposals of a most eligible man, but might possibly have formed new ties had circumstances been propitious—and neither did.

Anne's great speech will do for either of them: "All the privilege I claim for my own sex (it is not a very enviable one, you need not covet it) is that of loving longest, when existence or when hope is gone."[74] "Longest" she says (meaning "longer"); she does not say "forever".

If Anne were 'almost too good' for her creator, I suspect that it was more in the character of a sister; Jane Austen would have submitted less meekly to an Elizabeth Elliot, would have been less patient with the hypochondria of a Mary Musgrove. She had not, however, Anne's misfortune, of being the only amiable member of her family.

Anne was twenty-seven, the most mature of Jane Austen's heroines; Marianne Dashwood considered that a woman of that age could "never hope to feel or inspire affection again".[75] The autumnal setting with which her story begins does not suggest that (as Marianne might think) she has reached the autumn of life; but she has reached the autumn of youth.

For the first time, 'sensibility' in a heroine is wholly admirable. We were to laugh at Marianne and her dead leaves. Fanny Price presented a more difficult problem; we were to laugh, no doubt, at the idea of a Scottish monarch sleeping below the floor of the chapel at Sotherton, but our laughter was embarrassed and wry—it was too much like having to laugh at an adolescent *gaffe* of one's own. And when Fanny rhapsodized about the evergreen,[76] we did not know which way to look, and felt sincerely sorry for Mary Crawford. But Anne's sensibility is as adult as the rest of her personality. Her elegiac mood of 'desolate tranquillity'[77] is completely in harmony with 'the last smiles of the year upon the tawny leaves and withered hedges',[78] and with pre-romantic poetry; one regrets that she could not know Tennyson. Captain Benwick's easier and shallower emotions require 'dark blue seas' (so improbable at Lyme Regis in November), and the noisier poetry of 'Mr Scott and Lord Byron'.

Mrs Leavis has called this book an 'Anti-sense and Sensibility', and there is truth in the phrase; but perhaps one might rather say that there has been a reconcilement and, in Anne Elliot, Sense and Sensibility have kissed each other.

'How eloquent could Anne Elliot have been,—how eloquent, at least, were her wishes on the side of early warm attachment, and a cheerful confidence in futurity, against that over-anxious caution which seems to insult exertion and distrust Providence!—She had been forced into prudence in her youth, she learned romance as she grew older—the natural sequel of an unnatural beginning.'[79]

Captain Harville is Jane Austen's most charming portrait of the affectionate, domesticated naval officer. Sir Francis Austen recognized his making and contriving (his 'deediness') as a trait of his own. Otherwise the likeness must be very general. Captain Harville's emotional language reminds us less of the reserved Frank than of the expansive Charles (he is not given a Christian name; he could hardly have been called Charles as the name is given to four other characters in the book). Many models must have sat to Jane Austen for her few naval officers, and it would be rash to make too much of any suspected likeness.

At Lyme, Captain Harville opened his heart to Anne, in return for her kindness in drawing out Captain Benwick to talk. Lightly sketched in as he was, he was ready to Jane Austen's hand, and when she wished to rewrite the penultimate chapter, she could easily get the Musgroves to bring him to Bath. There he takes part with Anne in their great duet: 'a slight noise called their attention to Captain Wentworth's hitherto perfectly quiet division of the room. It was nothing more than that his pen had fallen down....'[80] The two beautiful voices of the double concerto have been interrupted by a thrilling note on the drum. When Captain Wentworth picks up his pen again, we may believe it is to write in a third part for himself, and the slow movement ends on a soaring crescendo of hope. It is the most beautiful and the most exciting love-scene in English fiction.

§7. The Cancelled Chapter

The denouement of Anne's story, related in the tenth and eleventh chapter of the second volume, is the last piece of her writing, apart from letters, and the vestigial *Sanditon*. She was dissatisfied with the original tenth chapter (which was then penultimate). 'She thought it tame and flat, and was desirous of producing something better. This weighed on her mind, the more so probably on account of the weak state of her health; so that one night she retired to rest in very low spirits. But such depression was little in accordance with her nature, and was soon shaken off. The next morning she awoke to more cheerful views and brighter inspirations: the sense of power revived; and imagination resumed its course. She cancelled the condemned chapter, and wrote two others, entirely different, in its stead.'[81]

Most fortunately the cancelled chapter has been preserved, affording us an unique opportunity of watching Jane Austen at her work of rewriting and revision—in fact, at her most characteristic work. We see her being both creative and critical.

Originally the story had a certain swiftness and simplicity, which she may have sacrificed with reluctance. Only the Crofts and Captain Wentworth himself brought the denouement about.

Anne was returning home, shaken by Mrs Smith's revelations, when Admiral Croft met her, near his own door, and insisted on taking her into the house to see his wife. Mrs Croft was with her mantua-maker, and the Admiral had at once to go out on business; he left Anne with Captain Wentworth, who was charged to give her a message from him and his wife. The message was a singular one: the Crofts had heard that Anne and Mr Elliot were to marry, and wished to express their willingness to give up Kellynch to the young Elliots, should that be their wish. "There is no truth in any such report",[82] said Anne—and they were reunited.

The explanation that, in the revised text, takes place in 'the comparatively quiet and retired gravel walk',[83] is now set in the Admiral's lodgings, where Anne (detained by the rain) remains to dinner. The Crofts (a little by Mrs Croft's contrivance) are a good deal out of the way—'gone upstairs to hear a noise, or downstairs to settle their accounts, or upon the landing place to trim a lamp'.[84]

In the revised text, it may be noted, a great deal of the explanation is altered from summary into direct speech; more sharpness and immediacy is given, though some readers still find it a little flat. Perhaps it is and should be flat—a quiet transition from 'the overplus of bliss'[85] towards a life of quiet happiness.

The scene at the *White Hart* is so wonderful, that there can be nothing for real regret; but there are beauties in the cancelled chapter that we are glad to have preserved, almost as variant readings. More is seen of the domestic life of those admirable Crofts; Captain Wentworth makes a feeling reference to Anne's friendship for them: "the Admiral is a man who can never be thought impertinent by one who knows him as you do";[86] and the hero is perhaps brought to life more fully here than anywhere else in the book. The paragraph following Anne's denial of the report must have been hard to sacrifice.

'He was a moment silent. She turned her eyes towards him for the first time since his re-entering the room. His colour was varying, and he was looking at her with all the power and keenness which she believed no other eyes than his possessed.'[87]

*

If she found the cancelled chapter tame, who can suppose that she was satisfied with Mrs Smith, Mr Elliot and Lady Russell? Had she had the time and the strength to return to them with the same transforming genius, and had she redone Louisa Musgrove's fall (sacrificing Mrs Lefroy as bravely as she had sacrificed her own love-story), *Persuasion* might have been the greatest of her novels; even in its present state it is the most moving.

A note on Sanditon

The twelve chapters later known in the Austen family as *Sanditon* were written between 27 January and 18 March 1817. The manuscript, first printed by Dr Chapman in 1925, is, according to his description, a first draft, much corrected by Jane Austen '*currente calamo*'. He contradicts the author of the *Memoir*, who believed that the later pages were written in pencil, 'probably when she was too weak to sit long at her desk', and afterwards written over in ink; 'The place at which pencil was used is in fact not much later than the middle; and the latter part of the manuscript shows no change in legibility or accuracy.'[1]

There has been a great deal of speculation about this fragment, most of which falls under two heads, summarized by Dr Chapman:[2] the harshness of satire and the tendency to caricature, and the greater awareness of the visible world. Moreover, no one has satisfactorily conjectured how the story was to go on.

The title might almost be that of Anna Lefroy's novel, *Who Is the Heroine?* Charlotte Heywood, a sensible young woman who goes to the rising watering-place, Sanditon, to stay with its promoter, Mr Parker, and his wife, almost certainly plays that role. But another candidate for it is Clara Brereton, the 'Cinderella' of the book; she lives as a companion with Lady Denham, the local 'great lady'—a person of much wealth and small education, who also is greatly interested in the development of Sanditon. Clara may be a second heroine.

Each group of heroine and chaperone has its appendages. Lady Denham is courted for her wealth by the nephew and niece of her second husband, Sir Edward Denham and his sister Esther. Sir Edward, we are told, intends to seduce Clara, his mind being corrupted by Richardson's novels; we may feel fairly confident that he will not get very far with her ('Let other pens dwell upon guilt and misery'), although we see her in a somewhat compromising situation at the end of the fragment. His stated intention, however, is something new—Jane Austen seems to be amused by it—and so is his character as an intellectual snob.

"I am no indiscriminate Novel-Reader. The mere Trash of the

common Circulating Library, I hold in the highest contempt. You will never hear me advocating those puerile Emanations which detail nothing but discordant Principles incapable of Amalgamation, or those vapid tissues of ordinary Occurrences from which no useful Deductions can be drawn.—In vain may we put them into a literary Alembic;—we distil nothing which can add to Science."[3]

Jane Austen was not only a novelist but, like all her family, a great reader of novels, and Sir Edward is not allowed to despise the novel with impunity; it appears that he thinks it should be a hand-book to seduction.

As an admirer of Romantic poetry, he tries to appear as a 'Man of Feeling', but he is evidently insincere and muddled. "Do you remember, said he, Scott's beautiful Lines on the Sea?—Oh! what a description they convey!—They are never out of my Thoughts when I walk here.—That Man who can read them unmoved must have the nerves of an Assassin!—Heaven defend me from meeting such a Man un-armed."[4] And Sir Edward cannot exactly recollect how the lines begin.

I fancy that Jane Austen may be drawing upon a part of her experience that she has not hitherto made use of, the London talk heard when she was staying with her brother Henry. It is perhaps not too fanciful to hear in Sir Edward an echo of a worthier person: 'I have been listening to dreadful Insanity.—It is Mr Haden's firm belief that a person *not* musical is fit for every sort of wickedness.'[5] I am afraid that Haden was quoting Shakespeare, and Jane Austen had failed to recognize the passage.

> *The man that hath no music in himself,*
> *Nor is not mov'd with concord of sweet sounds,*
> *Is fit for treasons, stratagems and spoils . . .'*

Mr and Mrs Parker have for their appendages a numerous family. There is the farcical group of hypochondriacs, Miss Susan and Miss Diana Parker, and their younger brother, Arthur; Diana is further distinguished by being a violent busybody, and Arthur by love of his food. Another brother, Sydney, a smart man-about-town, appears in the last few pages 'driving his servant in a very neat Carriage'.[6] He might, one suspects, have affinities with John Thorpe; we can be quite certain that he was not going to be the hero of the book, for Jane Austen could not have named a hero

'Sydney Parker'. The story is therefore exceptionally slow in beginning, for no hero has yet put in an appearance; he may, however, have been announced, as Sydney Parker was expecting to be joined at the hotel 'by a friend or two'. Perhaps the 'friend or two' were (or included) 'The Brothers', who (according to a family tradition) were to provide the title of the work;[7] one may imagine that (after various vicissitudes) one of them was united to Clara, and the other to Charlotte. Sydney Parker might easily have friends much superior to himself; I daresay one of them was a clergyman.

If it is true that the hero has yet to make an entrance, then, we can be assured that we really know nothing of the book, of its story or its moral atmosphere; we know only its social and geographic setting, and it is probable that we have met nearly all the minor characters. The enthusiasm of Mr Parker, the meddlesomeness of his sister Diana, the stinginess of Lady Denham, the machinations of Sir Edward, will all contribute to the 'distress' of the work. It is likely that a great deal of cutting would have been done, so that the real interest might not begin so late.

No one who accepts the view of Jane Austen's working habits that has been here set forth, need be disconcerted by this fragment. We may say that it is much inferior, not only to the six novels, but also to *Lady Susan* and *The Watsons*; and yet we have no need to say that it shows failing powers. It shows what her first drafts were like, before she had worked over them—with her, work was done on paper that many writers do first in their heads; she got down a rapid rough draft as a basis for future work, and no one should expect this to be a work of art. The harshness of the satire and the tendency to caricature are therefore just what we might have expected—a feature of her writing since schoolroom days. We cannot doubt that she intended to work on Diana Parker, Sir Edward and the rest, until they became plausible characters.

It is unfortunate that this fragment should be known as *Sanditon*; the name has influenced several critics to believe that Jane Austen was attempting something quite new, the bringing of a place to life. If it were certain that it should be called *The Brothers* (and no one can possibly suppose these to have been Thomas, Sydney and Arthur Parker), we should be better aware how small our knowledge is, and we should not magnify out of proportion the little we do know.

When Charlotte was first installed in her room at Trafalgar House, she 'found amusement enough in standing at her ample Venetian window, & looking over the miscellaneous foreground of unfinished Buildings, waving Linen, & tops of Houses, to the Sea, dancing and sparkling in Sunshine and Freshness'.[8] I am not convinced that there is anything in this often quoted passage that we could not have foretold from Emma, standing 'amused enough'[9] at the door of Ford's shop, or from the party at Lyme lingering 'as all must linger and gaze on a first return to the sea, who ever deserve to look on it at all'.[10] There seems no reason to expect that background should be more important in this book than it was in *Emma* or *Persuasion*.

More interesting is the famous *chiaroscuro* in the last chapter. 'Charlotte as soon as they entered the Enclosure, caught a glimpse over the pales of something White & Womanish in the field on the other side;—it was something which immediately brought Miss B. into her head—& stepping to the pales, she saw indeed—& very decidedly, in spite of the Mist; Miss B—seated, not far before her, at the foot of the bank which sloped down from the outside of the Paling & which a narrow Path seemed to skirt along;—Miss Brereton seated, apparently very composedly—& Sir E.D. by her side.'[11] This certainly seems an effect unique in Jane Austen's work, but one must hesitate to make too much of it: we know (alas) no more than Charlotte what was the significance of the scene, and we must therefore be entirely ignorant of the reasons for its presentation in this manner.

Moreover, it might well be an isolated effect. The symbolic use of background occurs only in the wood at Sotherton. It is not unnatural that a writer should once in his life strike a note that he does not happen (or care) to strike again.

The biographical criticism of this fragment (started off, as we saw, by a mis-statement on the part of the author of the *Memoir*) seems to me extremely dubious. I believe that, until ill-health forbade her to write, it did not much affect Jane Austen's writing. She believed that she was going to recover (and *Sanditon* was an undertaking that would demand at least eighteen months, if not more)—and after 18 March she wrote at least one lively letter. On or about that date she certainly had been 'very poorly',[12] and it was natural that she should break off for a time. Moreover, she had reached a point in her narrative (as I think) where even an author in robust health might have paused; she had set the scene, and in the next chapter (perhaps) the hero would have entered, and the story would have begun, and the serious effort of creation with it. By the end of March she was gravely ill[13] and unable to pick up the work again. Those who must have a personal story at all costs, may see a brave resistance to illness in her mockery of the hypochondriacs, but it is probably no more than a return to a subject which she thought she had not exhausted in the creation of Mr Woodhouse and Mary Musgrove.

To us, the greatest interest offered by *Sanditon* lies in the corrections in the manuscript; again we can see Jane Austen at work. We note that almost every addition or correction to Sir Edward's speeches heightens his absurdity: 'Unconquerable Decision' now becomes 'indomptible', and the 'sagacious' novel-reader (that is, Sir Edward himself) becomes 'anti-puerile'. It would, we may be sure, have cost Jane Austen many a pang to tone down this figure of fun into a plausible character. And we may also be grateful for Mr Parker's speech: '*We* have all the Grandeur of the Storm, with less real danger, because the Wind meeting with nothing to oppose or confine it around our house, simply rages & passes on.'[14]

The Letters

Jane Austen was not one of the great letter-writers of the world; with those who were consciously great letter-writers, it may be said at once that she did not compete. 'I have now attained the true art of letter-writing,' she wrote, 'which we are always told, is to express on paper exactly what one would say to the same person by word of mouth; I have been talking to you almost as fast as I could the whole of this letter.'[1] It is in the schoolroom, I suppose, that we are told that sort of thing; this is not how Cicero, or the younger Pliny or Horace Walpole understood 'the gentlest art'.

Neither the vanity nor the anguish of the great letter-writers was hers, nor their richness of subject-matter, nor their need.

Horace Walpole and Madame de Sévigné were professional letter-writers, in that their letters were their chief or only form of self-expression. They were also gazetteers, reporting to the provinces or abroad, with infinite gaiety and liveliness, the doings of London or Paris, and news which could not yet have reached their correspondents from another source. The daily newspaper, the weekly periodical and the wireless have, no doubt, killed this kind of letter-writing for ever. We are far removed from a time in which the death of a general in action could find its best historian in a mother writing to an absent daughter. Jane Austen is nearer to us in that such subjects are not hers; moreover, she had her true form of self-expression in the novel. She would not use her letters for this purpose; she was too modest and too considerate of others. Even in our own age, we sometimes resent the outpourings of ill-conditioned correspondents; in the reign of George III we should have had to pay for them.

With those writers whose literary reputation entirely rests on their letters (Pliny, Madame de Sévigné, Horace Walpole), we may link those glorious letter-writers, the poets, who have found in their letters an unique opportunity for using the prose which their more exacting craft has so finely tempered. Jane Austen, whose talent for verse was not much above the average, is poles apart from that company that includes Gray, Cowper, Keats, Byron, the Brownings and Hopkins.

143

She was not an educator, like Chesterfield. When, exceptionally, she advises one niece (Fanny Knight) on her affairs of the heart, or another (Anna Lefroy) on the construction of a novel, her letters become quite unusually interesting. She was not a traveller, like Gray or Byron. Above all, she was not a lover, she was not a solitary, she was not a malcontent.

It is sometimes suggested that her sister, Cassandra, was not a very inspiring correspondent; I think this is a mistaken estimate of the probabilities of the case. The prosaic nature of the letters is the result of the normality of the sisters' relationship. Another sister would not have received better letters; Cassandra might, in different circumstances, have received letters that were far more touching. If she had married, and gone into Shropshire, the letters would have filled an urgent need to keep their close affection alive. They were normally together, and their letters needed only to bridge gaps in a shared life, and to communicate news and gossip. Moreover, though there was between the two women of the family a deep love, a close intimacy, and a mutual need of each other greater than their need for any of the brothers, the largeness of the family must affect the intensity of the relationship. Jane Austen had no sister but Cassandra, but she was not only Cassandra's sister; she may (in a different way) have loved Henry as much or more, while Edward may (in some ways) have had the first place with Cassandra.

The letters, therefore, cannot compare with those that are the only common life of friends apart (such as those from Madame de Sévigné to her daughter during their long separations, those between Horace Walpole and Sir Horace Mann, or between Hopkins and Dixon or Bridges). And (as in all happy instances of the fraternal relationship) there was absolute confidence in a mutual affection, and certainty that absences were only temporary—though a 'Kentish visit' might last an unconscionable time. There is never the pang of parting that often makes the letters of Madame de Sévigné to Françoise-Marguerite de Grignan so painful—and these are love-letters, as much as those of Dorothy Osborne to Sir William Temple, of Gray to Charles Louis Victor de Bonstetten, of Keats to Fanny Brawne, or of Katherine Mansfield to Middleton Murry. When apart, the sisters did not suffer from loneliness; one was at home, surrounded by objects of affection, and the other was visiting a much loved brother. Their separations (chiefly motivated by unselfish consideration for others) were of the sort that wise people often deliberately cultivate for the sake of the enrichment of their life together.

It is sometimes conjectured that Jane Austen's letters to her brother Henry may have been of especial interest; she must certainly have discussed the business of publication with him, and may have written to him about problems arising from her art. In any case it is greatly to be regretted that we have no letters to that brother whose liveliness must have put her on her mettle as a correspondent (her letters to Frank are her worst); but it is unlikely that she ever wrote with such ease as to her sister.

The letters are of infinite value to us because of their minute revelation of the background and everyday life of a woman of genius. And, even if Jane Austen had written nothing else, we should find in them an unique picture of upper middle-class life in Kent and Hampshire during twenty-one years, in several large country houses, parsonages, and small houses in country towns or villages. We should be fascinated by the writer, and thirst to know more about her.

If the letters were approached in this way, they would have a higher reputation; those who come to them hoping to find some of the writer's best work (as they find in the letters of Katherine Mansfield or D. H. Lawrence), are doomed to disappointment. And yet they are a part of the circumstances that fostered and conditioned her genius; they record the world that was her subject-matter, and they are addressed to the public that was peculiarly hers and set her tone—many of them were 'epistles general', to be read, in full or in part, to the family circle, the readers and critics whom she most wished to please.

They were not written for us; had she foreseen how they would be published, annotated and criticized, we may be very sure that Cassandra would not have allowed one of them to survive. We know that she had already edited them. Their niece Caroline says of Jane Austen: 'her letters to Aunt Cassandra were, I daresay, open and confidential. My Aunt looked them over and burnt the greater part as she told me three or four years before her own death. She left or gave some as legacies to the nieces, but of those that I have seen several had portions cut out.'[2] She burnt, one may presume, what she regarded as personal and sacred confidences that were only for herself, leaving to her nieces relics of a beloved aunt, and a fascinating record of their family history. It is also probable that she excised passages that were particularly unfavourable to their parents—we may be thankful that so much escaped her scissors or the fire. Modesty, no doubt, made her burn her own letters—a bitter loss to us.

We are therefore obliged to criticize the letters in a slightly different manner from that which we should use towards works that are addressed to us—and such works may include diaries, when the diarist had an eye to posterity. We should put ourselves in the position of Cassandra, and ask whether these letters would have been a delight to receive; if we think they would (and who can think otherwise?) the writer has achieved what she set out to do. The charge of triviality disappears; details of a coquelicot feather or haricot mutton would have been interesting to Cassandra, for whom alone they were intended. And the other charge that is sometimes made, that of bad taste, has no meaning—taste (good or bad) presupposes some social standards, that do not exist when one is talking to oneself, or to a sister who is an *alter ego*.

That does not mean that we may not also stand a little further back, and look at the personality revealed in the letters, and see how we like it. Here we have the artless chatter of the private self; elsewhere we have the carefully wrought productions of the writing self. It is reasonable to try to put them together. Most candid readers will not find it an impossible task, and will be delighted with the composite portrait of a brave, observant, amusing, affectionate and high-spirited woman.

Those who have taken the opposite view are in a minority, but they have expressed their opinions very forcibly; moreover there are among them people for whose judgement we generally feel respect, notably Mr E. M. Forster. 'Triviality,' he says, 'varied by touches of ill breeding and of sententiousness characterizes these letters as a whole, particularly the earlier letters.'[3]

It is a painful thing when our friends fall out—and such friends as Jane Austen and E. M. Forster. We can have no doubt where our loyalty lies, but, though we must take her side, we shall wish to let him down as lightly as we can.

Fortunately, he has given us every help. We should not have been so impertinent as to call him uncritical, but he himself tells us that he is an uncritical worshipper of Jane Austen's novels; it would be equally impertinent to doubt his word. The idolatrous worshippers of the novels (as it has been suggested throughout this book) absorb them, but do not really read them; they do not know what the novels are like, nor what they tell us about their author. The conventional, anachronistic picture of Jane Austen is that of a refined Victorian lady, who (almost by direct inspiration) was a perfect artist; in her cult is combined a reverence due, among women, only to the Blessed Virgin, with the adoring affection given to the dearest possible of maiden aunts. All this has very little to do with the person who lived, as a lively girl and as a shrewd young woman, in the reign of George III. In the letters she is revealed almost beyond the possibility of misunderstanding; though I have no doubt at all that some obstinate readers manage to distort them, so that they fit in with the cult picture. An honest worshipper, like Mr Forster, might well get a few shocks. His surprise at meeting the real Jane Austen, perhaps, may be the reason that he is much less than fair to her. 'Neither Emma Woodhouse nor Anne Elliot nor even Frank Churchill or Mary Crawford dominates her pen. The controls are rather Lydia Bennet, Mrs Jennings and Sir Thomas Bertram, a bizarre and inauspicious combine.'[4]

Sir Thomas, I suppose, wrote the letters of condolence. Such letters should not be preserved; anyone with a good memory will blush with shame for those which he has written, and with vicarious shame for many which he has received. On the whole, those that are conventional and even pompous are probably the best; other people's grief is better saluted by an impersonal and respectful gesture of sympathy, rather than by the obtrusion of our own sensibility. It could have been Sir Thomas, or even Mr Collins, who wrote to Philadelphia Walter on her father's death: 'But the very circumstance which at present enhances your loss, must gradually reconcile you to it the better; the Goodness which made him valuable on Earth, will make him Blessed in Heaven.—This consideration must bring comfort to yourself, to my Aunt, & to all his family and friends. . . .'[5] A twentieth century young woman, I daresay, would have written a letter full of whimsical, affectionate, half-humorous reminiscences of 'darling Uncle Bill'.

Even Christians, in this post-Christian world, find it difficult to place themselves imaginatively in even such an age of faith as that in which Jane Austen lived, and automatically to think of death as she thought of it. For her (as for his family) the first point of interest was where William Walter had gone, and not that Seale, near Sevenoaks, would know him no more. Sir Thomas, however, as we know, 'thought justly'.

No sister, I daresay, would now write, as she wrote to her brother Frank, after their father's death: 'The Serenity of the Corpse is most delightful!'[6] And yet this would be to her brother a valuable sign of a peaceful and Christian end. Mr Forster complains that in her letters on the occasion there is 'none of the outpour' that we find in Cassandra's touching letters to Fanny Knight in 1817. The death of an elderly father is not the same unnatural and inconsolable loss as the death of a younger sister. Jane Austen was trying as far as she could to spare the 'affectionate heart' of a brother who was unavoidably absent; Cassandra was afraid of breaking Fanny's heart by her outpour.

Sir Thomas for death, Mrs Jennings (I suppose) for birth. 'The facts', Mr Forster says, 'were not her facts'; and yet Jane Austen and Mrs Jennings knew more about expectant motherhood than any man outside the medical profession is likely to know. Again, the historical approach is necessary; it was no age of planned parenthood or of twilight sleep. Childbirth was not 'holy and beautiful', but annual, frightening and frequently fatal. You might make jokes about it, but it was in the way in which we make jokes about bombs. Mr Forster speaks of ill-breeding, and lack of feeling, but look at the facts. 'Anna has not a chance of escape', Jane Austen wrote to Fanny Knight. 'Poor animal, she will be worn out before she is thirty.—I am very sorry for her.—Mrs Clement too is in that way again. I am quite tired of so many Children—Mrs Benn has a 13th.'[8]

Men should be careful when they write about pregnancy to avoid the complacent tone in which clergymen and old women used to talk about conscription for military service, before the dangers of war came so near to everyone. Katherine Mansfield (who had gone through it) was understandably indignant with D. H. Lawrence; she wished that he could give birth to a baby, and have rather a bad time with it—he would not then write such nonsense about 'trills in the bowels'.

If we are imaginative enough to read the letters in the same spirit that the author writ, Jane Austen's occasional savagery about motherhood becomes perfectly intelligible to us as a sympathetic reaction from the fate of her married friends. The jest about Mrs Hall of Sherborne's baby should distress no one who realizes that Mrs Hall was through her trouble, and 'some weeks before she expected'.[9] Very likely she had many more children.

Lydia Bennet, no doubt, would write of love and marriage—but I cannot find her in the letters as a 'control'. If she occurs, it is in a contemptuous reference to Miss Fletcher, whose apology for not writing to Lucy Lefroy was that everybody whom Lucy had known in Canterbury had now left it. 'By *Everybody*, I suppose Miss Fletcher means that a new set of Officers have arrived there.'[10] Though Miss Fletcher had two pleasing traits in her character: 'Namely, she admires Camilla, & drinks no cream in her Tea', it is not surprising that, when she and Jane Austen were 'very thick', Jane Austen was 'the thinnest of the two'—a thing Lydia could never have said.

Jane Austen had no dislike for officers, but they do not loom large in her letters. She enjoyed a ball, and its subsequent *post mortem*—but so did Fanny Price. There can be no doubt that she flirted competently and amusingly—so did Elizabeth Bennet. She was a jolly, healthy, clever and extremely attractive girl—and so was Cassandra, to whom she was writing. Such letters need no apology; Jane Austen was not, at twenty-one, a cloistered, dedicated writer—and a good thing that she was not, for her novels would then have been unspeakably dull. Mr Forster finds her hard —but if she had written anything tender (and she probably did) Cassandra would not have let it survive for him to read. We know enough about her (though all too little) to be aware that her attitude to marriage was particularly delicate.

Births, deaths and marriages, however, were not the staple of Jane Austen's news; neither were dress, balls, nor officers. Plans, domestic details, thumbnail sketches of a great many people— these are what the reader of the letters chiefly remembers, and, above all, the frequent felicity of phrase. Sometimes Mary Crawford (at her best) holds the pen, and sometimes Henry Tilney, for there is a 'niceness' about the language—but more often it is the unmistakeable writing of Jane Austen herself.

'I am very much flattered by your commendation of my last letter, for I write only for fame, and without any view to pecuniary emolument.'[11]

'. . . If the Pearsons were not at home, I should inevitably fall a Sacrifice to the arts of some Fat Woman who would make me drunk with Small Beer.'[12]

'You express so little anxiety about my being murdered under Ash Park Copse by Mr Hulbert's servant, that I have a great mind not to tell you whether I was or not, and shall only say that I did not return home that night or the next. . . .'[13]

'I am glad you recollected to mention your being come home. My heart began to sink within me when I had got so far through your Letter without its being mentioned. I was dreadfully afraid that you might be detained at Winchester by severe illness, confined to your Bed perhaps & quite unable to hold a pen, & only dating from Steventon in order, with a mistaken sort of tenderness, to deceive me.—But now I have no doubt of your being at home, I am sure you would not say it so seriously unless it actually were so!'[14]

This is a writer's playfulness; the mockery of the epistolary novel and of the afflicted heroine place such passages with the juvenile parodies. Elsewhere in the letters are skits on Mrs Piozzi,[15] and that 'strictly moral' novelist, Mrs Hunter of Norwich.[16]

Other playfulness, more particularly Jane Austen's own, constantly delights the reader of the letters, as it must have first delighted the recipient. If it is picked out of its context, the selector feels guilty of what Dr Chapman calls 'solemn absurdity'[17]—but it may be attempted.

(Of the new tables ordered for Steventon) 'They are both covered with green baize & send their best love.'[18]

'Mr Peter Debary has declined Deane curacy; he wishes to be settled nearer London. A foolish reason!, as if Deane were not near London in comparison of Exeter or York.—Take the whole world through, & he will find many more places at a greater distance from London than Deane, than he will at a less.—What does he think of Glencoe or Lake Katherine?'[19]

(Of her brother Frank) 'Poor fellow! to wait from the middle of November to the end of December, & perhaps longer! it must be sad work!—Especially in a place where the ink is so abominably pale.'[20]

We plan having a steady Cook, & a young giddy Housemaid, with a sedate, middle aged Man, who is to undertake the double

office of Husband to the former & sweetheart to the latter—no
Children of course to be allowed on either side.'[21]

Pleasant people abound in the Letters: kind elder women, like
Mrs Knight and Mrs Lefroy; contemporaries, such as the Misses
Bigg and Martha Lloyd; charming young relations, like James
Edward Austen, and Fanny Knight and her brothers. The prevail-
ing tone is kindly, and it is hard to sympathize with those critics
who are shocked at occasional touches of malice and asperity.
'Follies and nonsense, whims and inconsistencies *do* divert me, I
own, and I laugh at them whenever I can';[22] admirers of Elizabeth Bennet should not be distressed to find her creator behaving
in the same way. 'For what do we live, but to make sport for our
neighbours, and laugh at them in our turn?'[23] asked Mr Bennet.
It would be a sad thing to have to endure a large circle of acquaintance without the compensation of picking them to pieces with our
friends.

The thumbnail sketches may sometimes be sharp, but there is
never a trace of peevishness, envy or ill-temper—none of the
superiority of Horace Walpole, the snarl of D. H. Lawrence, or the
grouch of Katherine Mansfield.

(Of the Debary girls) 'I was as civil to them as their bad breath
would allow me.'[24]

(Of the adulterous Miss Twistleton) '. . . she was highly rouged,
& looked rather quietly and contentedly silly than anything
else.'[25]

(Of the Lances) '. . . we found only Mrs Lance at home, and
whether she boasts any offspring besides a grand pianoforte did
not appear. . . . They live in a handsome style and are rich, and
she seemed to like to be rich, and we gave her to understand that
we were far from being so; she will soon feel therefore that we are
not worth her acquaintance.'[26]

(Of Miss Payne) 'She told us a great deal about her friend Lady
Cath. Brecknell, who is most happily married—& Mr Brecknell
is very religious, and has got black whiskers.'[27]

(Of Mr Lushington) 'He is quite an M.P.—very smiling, with
an exceeding good address, & readiness of Language.—I am rather
in love with him.—I dare say he is ambitious & Insincere.'[28]

'The Webbs are really gone. When I saw the Waggons at the
door, & thought of all the trouble they must have in moving, I

began to reproach myself for not having liked them better—but since the Waggons have disappeared, my Conscience has been closed again—& I am excessively glad they are gone.'[29]

'All of you that are well enough to look, are now passing your Judgements I suppose on Mrs John Butler; & 'is she pretty? or is she not?' is the knotty question. Happy Woman! to stand the gaze of a neighbourhood as the Bride of such a pink-faced, simple young Man!'[30]

More deeply interesting to us are the references to 'mixed' characters. 'Mrs J.A.' was rather slatternly: 'Mary does not manage matters in such a way as to make me want to lay in myself';[31] she had some of Mary Musgrove's feeling that she was slighted, and not a little of Mrs Norris's love of interfering, she was 'in the main *not* a liberal-minded woman'[32]—but could do some things 'in the kindest manner'. Anna, her step-daughter, was self-willed, and not absolutely straightforward about little things—but she had a great affection for her aunt. If I were to make a personal criticism of Jane Austen (and I do not think that our knowledge of the facts is sufficient to justify it), I should feel tempted to complain of her discussing Anna's faults so freely with Fanny, another niece, and Anna's younger contemporary. But posterity, which knows Lady Knatchbull's disagreeable letter, must feel some prejudice in favour of Mrs Ben Lefroy, whose posthumous love for her aunt cannot be doubted; alas, she proved it in a way most unfortunate for us, by destroying the novel upon which Jane Austen had advised her, because she had no more heart in it after her aunt was dead.

The letters have a life and an interest altogether superior to that commonly found in the reminiscences of authors. They are much given to 'name-dropping'. Glance at the index, and you will find that they have met (say) Virginia Woolf, Lady Oxford and André Gide; turn up the page, and they have nothing of consequence to say about them. Jane Austen (happily unaware of the fact), never met anyone of an eminence approaching her own (though she might, I daresay, have seen Newman in the street in Alton as a boy); she has seen something of interest in a vast number of unimportant people, and has put it down for Cassandra and others, and has given a small immortality to Mr Deedes, Mr Robert Mascall, Mrs Digweed and so many more. This is creation.

Though unlucky in love and (for many years) disappointed in

authorship, though socially almost a nonentity, while mentally the superior of everyone about her, she never gives way to grumbling, whining or vanity. The letters are those of a woman who did her duty in that state of life into which it had pleased God to call her, and there found her happiness.

Textual Notes

Northanger Abbey (p. 207)

' "You feel, I suppose, that, in losing Isabella, you lose half yourself; you feel a void in your heart which nothing else can occupy. Society is becoming irksome; and as for the amusements in which you were wont to share in Bath, the very idea of them without her is abhorrent." '

I am sure Henry Tilney said: "Society is become irksome."

Sense and Sensibility (p. 221)

'John Dashwood was really far from being sorry to see his sisters again; it rather gave them satisfaction; and his inquiries after their mother were respectful and attentive.'

them should surely be emended to *him*.

Mansfield Park (p. 171)

' "Dr Grant is ill," said she, with mock solemnity. "He has been ill ever since; he did not eat any of the pheasant today. He fancied it tough—sent away his plate—and has been suffering ever since." '

This would read better: "He has been ill ever since he did not eat any of the pheasant today."

ib. (pp. 328–9)

'Now she was angry. Some resentment did arise at a perseverance so selfish and ungenerous. Here was again a want of delicacy and regard for others which had formerly so struck and disgusted her. Here was again a something of the same Mr Crawford whom she had so reprobated before. Now evidently was there a gross want of feeling and humanity where his own pleasure was concerned—And, alas! how always known no principle to supply as a duty what the heart was deficient in.'

Dr Chapman (p. 548) calls this a 'certainly corrupt place', and suggests as a 'plausible correction' that by Professor Henry Jackson '(who did not remember if it were his own or not)'—*And, alas! now all was known no principle* . . . . .
I do not find this plausible; it could hardly be said, at this point, that *all was known*. I am not sure that the place is corrupt, though admittedly the author was expressing herself somewhat inelegantly. I think she meant to say: *And, alas! How* (well it had) *always* (been) *known* (to Fanny that there was in Henry) *no principle.* . . . I think the words, even as they stand, convey that meaning.

154

Persuasion (p. 70)

' "I have crossed the Atlantic four times, and have been once to the East Indies, and back again; and only once, besides being in different places about home—Cork, and Lisbon, and Gibraltar." '

Another case for re-punctuation: "I have crossed the Atlantic four times, and have been once to the East Indies, and back again, and only once; besides. . . ."

Notes

NORTHANGER ABBEY

1. *Life*, p. 96
2. Leavis, I., p. 63
3. *Life*, p. 174
4. *Letters*, 67
5. *Memoir*, p. 138
6. *Letters*, 141
7. *P.*, pp. 275–9
8. Lascelles, p. 48
9. *N. A.*, p. xii
10. Leavis, loc. cit.
11. Lascelles, pp. 61 ff.
12. *N. A.*, p. 13
13. *Letters*, 6
14. *N. A.*, p. 14
15. ib., p. 16
16. Lascelles, p. 60
17. *Emmeline, the Orphan of the Castle* (1785)
18. *N. A.*, p. 16
19. ib., p. 18
20. ib., p. 19
21. ib., pp. 26–7
22. ib., p. 49
23. ib., p. 75
24. ib., p. 53
25. ib., p. 90
26. ib., p. 60
27. ib., p. 49
28. ib., pp. 157–8
29. *P.*, pp. 285–290
30. *N. A.*, p. 164
31. ib., p. 173
32. ib., p. 179
33. ib., p. 181
34. ib., p. 182
35. ib., p. 186
36. ib., p. 187
37. ib., pp. 187–9
38. ib., p. 193
39. *Letters*, 37
40. *N. A.*, pp. 197–8
41. ib., pp. 199–200
42. ib., p. 207
43. ib., p. 34
44. ib., p. 247
45. ib., p. 251
46. Leavis, I., p. 71
47. Lascelles, p. 63
48. *N. A.*, p. 94
49. ib., p. 243
50. see p. 61
51. *N. A.*, p. 95
52. ib., p. 166
53. ib., p. 175
54. ib., p. 178
55. ib., p. 184
56. ib., p. 103
57. ib., p. 129
58. ib., p. 80
59. ib., p. 187
60. ib., p. 196
61. ib., p. 197

SENSE AND SENSIBILITY

1. *Life*, p. 96
2. *Life*, p. 80
3. Chapman, p. 42
4. *Memoir*, p. 49

NOTES

5. Biographical Notice, *N. A.*, p. 4
Letters, 134. Letters of Henry's, preserved in the *Life*, are pompous and grandiloquent
6. Lascelles, pp. 15–16
7. *S. S.*, p. 98
8. *S. S.*, p. 18
9. *P. P.*, pp. 400–7
10. *N. P.*, pp. 553–6
11. *Letters*, 70
12. Leavis, I., p. 85
13. *S. S.*, p. 22
14. *N. A.*, p. 72. The homonymity between Eleanor and Elinor is perhaps not fortuitous.
15. *S. S.*, p. 47
16. ib., p. 83
17. *P.*, pp. 100–1
18. ibid.
19. *S. S.*, p. 56
20. ibid.
21. *S. S.*, pp. 47–8
22. ib., pp. 93–4
23. ib., p. 263
24. ib., p. 359
25. ib., p. 18
26. ib., p. 49
27. ib., p. 81
28. Lascelles, pp. 65–6
29. *S. S.*, p. 319
30. ib., p. 154
31. ib., p. 155
32. ib., p. 161
33. ib., p. 165
34. ib., p. 177
35. ib., p. 76
36. ib., p. 184
37. ib., p. 180
38. ib., p. 182
39. *Conversations in Ebury Street*, chap. xvii
40. *Abinger Harvest*
41. *The Four Loves* (London, 1960)
42. *S. S.*, p. 210
43. ib., p. 345
44. ib., p. 320
45. ib., p. 322
46. ib., p. 209
47. ib., p. 322
48. *M. P.*, p. 465
49. *S. S.*, pp. 201–2
50. Leavis, I., p. 85
51. *S. S.*, p. 94
52. ib., p. 127
53. ib., p. 144
54. *Summa Theologica* 2ᵃ 2ᵃᵉ qu. 153, art. 5
55. *S. S.*, p. 155
56. ib., p. 346
57. Leavis I., p. 85
58. ib., p. 83
59. *S. S.*, pp. 345–6
60. ib., p. 346
61. Leavis I., p. 86
62. *S. S.*, p. 264
63. ib., pp. 87–8
64. ib., p. 123
65. ib., p. 275
66. ib., p. 198
67. ib., p. 247
68. ib., pp. 104–5
69. ib., p. 91
70. ib., p. 251
71. ib., p. 369
72. ib., p. 374
73. ib., p. 91
74. ib., p. 292
75. ib., p. 91
76. ib., p. 93
77. ib., p. 260
78. ib., p. 277

79. ib., p. 320
80. ib., p. 350
81. ib., p. 194
82. ib., p. 378
83. *M. P.*, p. 470
84. *S. S.*, p. 25
85. ib., p. 87
86. ib., p. 123
87. ib., p. 13
88. ib., pp. 146-9
89. ib., p. 263
90. ib., p. 367
91. ib., p. 274

92. ib., p. 367
93. *Sense and Sensibility: An Assessment,* by Christopher Gillie (Essays in Criticism IX. i., pp. 6 ff.)
94. *S. S.*, p. 197
95. *P. P.*, p. 236
96. Leavis, I., p. 85
97. Chapman, pp. 184-7
98. *S. S.*, pp. 378-9
99. ib., p. 379
100. ib., p. 248
101. ib., p. 213

PRIDE AND PREJUDICE

1. *Life*, pp. 96-8
2. Lascelles, p. 14
3. Leavis, I., p. 63. It is just possible that a kind of compromise may be found between these two plausible (and equally unsupported) opinions. Perhaps the *First Impressions* finished in 1797 was indeed in direct narrative, but was a recension of an earlier draft in letter-form, of whose existence we have now no evidence. Cassandra's note may thus refer only to novels in narrative form; it is not to her that we owe our knowledge of the epistolary *Elinor and Marianne.* Jane Austen, as a girl of twenty-two, might be more confident than she later became; in later life she would not have finished a new novel in August and have allowed her father to offer it to a publisher only three months later.
4. *Letters*, 17
5. ib., 21
6. *Life*, p. 243
7. *Letters*, 74.1.
8. ib., 76
9. ib., 78
10. Lascelles, p. 31
11. *P. P.*, p. xiii
12. I follow Dr Chapman's chronology, *P. P.*, pp. 400-7
13. *S. S.*, p. 46
14. *N. A.*, p. 5
15. *P. P.*, p. 408
16. Leavis, I., pp. 71-5
17. *P. P.*, p. 289
18. *Evelina*, letter xxxix
19. *P. P.*, p. 112
20. *Evelina*, letter lxxx
21. *M. W.*, p. 91; Leavis, I., p. 70

22. *M. W.*, pp. 156–160
23. Leavis, I., pp. 67–8
24. *M. W.*, p. 344
25. *Letters*, 99
26. ib., 58
27. ib., 76
28. ib., 78
29. *P. P.*, p. 24
30. ib., p. 383
31. *A Note on Jane Austen* (Essays in Criticism, IV., pp. 359–371)
32. Leavis, I., p. 73
33. *Life*, p. 74
34. This was very likely an event of unique importance in her life.
    'Cassandra thought him worthy to possess and likely to win her sister's love.' *Memoir*, pp. 28–9
35. *Life*, pp. 92–3
36. *Letters*, 56
37. *P. P.*, p. 135
38. ib., p. 144
39. ib., p. 149
40. ib., p. 152
41. ib., p. 154
42. ib., p. 158
43. ib., p. 187
44. ib., p. 265
45. ib., p. 208
46. ib., p. 209
47. ib., pp. 212–3
48. ib., p. 226
49. ib., p. 232
50. ib., p. 237
51. ib., p. 263
52. ib., p. 265
53. ib., p. 28
54. *E.*, p. 7
55. *P. P.*, p. 43
56. ib., p. 18
57. ib., p. 27
58. cit. *Jane Austen* by Sylvia Townsend Warner (British Council and National Book League, 1951), p. 19
59. *P. P.*, p. 36
60. ib., p. 37
61. ib., p. 198
62. ib., p. 179
63. ib., p. 231
64. *Letters*, 90
65. *P. P.*, p. 309
66. *N. A.*, p. 198
67. *M. W.*, p. 435
68. *P. P.*, p. 90
69. *P. P.*, p. 102
70. ib., p. 115
71. ib., p. 121
72. ib., p. 69
73. Leavis, I., p. 74
74. *M. W.*
75. *P. P.*, p. 44
76. *M. W.*, pp. 391–2
77. *Letters*, 86
78. *P. P.*, p. 23
79. ib., pp. 51–2
80. *Scrutiny*, xiii, 2, pp. 101–2
81. *Some Principles of Fiction*, p. 83
82. *P. P.*, p. 60
83. ib., p. 176
84. ib., p. 181
85. *M. P.*, p. 468
86. *P. P.*, p. 318

MANSFIELD PARK

1. *Life*, p. 290
2. *Letters*, 76
3. *Letters*, 92
4. Introduction to *M. P.* (R.W.C.), p. xi
5. *Memoir*, pp. 26–7
6. cit. Chapman, p. 127
7. Leavis, II., p. 121 n. Henry had courted Eliza 'for more than two years', *Life*, p. 107.
8. cit. Chapman, p. 128
9. Leavis, II, *passim*
10. *Letters*, 57. It is possible that the reference is to Elizabeth's brother Henry Bridges, but Dr Chapman thinks Henry Austen is intended.
11. *M. W.*, p. 311
12. Leavis, II
13. Lascelles, pp. 13–14
14. Leavis, I., pp. 67–8
15. *M. W.*, pp. 156–160
16. *Letters*, 31. Mrs J. A. 'Enjoyed Mrs Norris particularly' (Opinions, *M. W.*, pp. 431–2).
17. *Memoir*, p. 12
18. *Letters*, p. 49
19. Leavis, II, p. 133
20. *Letters*, 87
21. *Memoir*, p. 13. 'On a moderate estimate, eighty per cent of the heroes are called Henry.' J. M. S. Tomkins; *The Popular Novel in England*, 1770-1800 (London, 1932), p. 57 n. But good Mr Woodhouse's

name was Henry: 'A proof how unequally the gifts of Fortune are bestowed.'
22. Leavis, II, pp. 134–6
23. *Letters*, 52
24. *Letters*, 36
25. *M. P.*, p. 333
26. ib., p. 425
27. Leavis, II, pp. 137–8
28. *M. P.*, p. 55
29. ib., p. 333
30. ib., p. 339
31. ib., p. 449
32. ib., pp. 553–6
33. Leavis, II, pp. 122–4
34. *M. P.*, p. 450
35. *M. W.*, p. 313
36. *M. P.*, p. 470
37. *N. A.*, p. 281
38. *M. P.*, p. 461
39. *Letters*, 92
40. *Letters*, 93
41. Introduction to *Mansfield Park* (World's Classics edit.)
42. *M. P.*, pp. 63–4
43. ib., p. 294
44. ib., p. 359
45. ib., p. 143
46. ib., p. 147
47. ib., p. 402
48. ib., p. 147
49. ib., p. 467. Fanny comes near to recognizing an engagement between them (p. 441).
50. *Letters*, 101
51. *M. P.*, p. 115
52. ib., p. 123
53. ib., p. 467

54. *Letters,* 101
55. *M. P.*, p. 357. *Pace* Dr C. S. Lewis (*Studies in Words*, pp. 83–5) I think Mary means 'Wretched girl!' rather than "You are a prime one!" Mrs Price means 'wretched' when she says: "What a sad fire we have got" (p. 379) and that 'Portsmouth was a sad place' (p. 401)— but, unlike Mary, she intends no humour. Perhaps, however, she gives some sanction to the word, and it is not so reprehensible as some of Mary's severer critics think.
56. ib., p. 359
57. ib., p. 359
58. ib., p. 361
59. ib., p. 393
60. ib., p. 374
61. ib., p. 282
62. ib., p. 433
63. *Letters,* 40
64. Lascelles, p. 175
65. *M. P.*, p. 424
66. ib., p. 434
67. ib., p. 436
68. ib., p. 453
69. ib., p. 455
70. ib., p. 470
71. *Letters,* 18
72. *A Treatise on the Novel*, pp. 55 and nn.
73. *M. P.*, pp. 468–9
74. ib., p. 469
75. ib., p. 465
76. ib., p. 56
77. ib., p. 85
78. ib., pp. 85–6
79. ib., p. 62
80. ib., p. 84
81. ib., p. 91
82. ib., p. 88
83. ib., p. 91
84. ib., p. 94
85. ib., p. 99
86. ib., p. 102
87. ib., p. 244
88. ib., p. 124
89. ib., p. 125
90. ib., p. 180
91. ib., p. 40
92. ib., p. 137
93. ib., p. 169
94. ib., p. 358
95. ib., p. 164
96. ib., p. 170
97. ib., p. 163
98. ib., p. 172
99. *Letters,* 92
100. *M. P.*, p. 197
101. ib., p. 205
102. ib., p. 219
103. Leavis, I., p. 68
104. ibid.
105. *M. P.*, p. 193
106. ib., p. 162
107. ib., pp. 229–30
108. ib., p. 231
109. ib., p. 235
110. *Letters,* 38
111. *M. P.*, p. 262
112. *The Common Reader* (First Series), p. 178
113. *M. P.*, p. 369
114. ib., p. 413
115. ib., pp. 431–2
116. ib., p. 439
117. *Letters,* 18
118. *P.*, p. 33
119. *M. P.*, p. 473
120. Leavis, II., p. 134

121. *M. P.*, p. 10
122. ib., p. 313
123. ib., p. 463
124. ib., p. 88
125. ib., p. 111
126. *Memoir*, p. 16. Family tradition tended to identify William with Charles, and 'up to the day of his death there is one entry never absent from the diary of Charles Austen—"Read the Lessons of the Day." ' *Jane Austen's Sailor Brothers* by J. H. Hubback and Edith C. Hubback (London 1906), p. 115.
127. *M. P.*, p. 463
128. ib., p. 466
129. ib., p. 361
130. ib., p. 461
131. ib., p. 463
132. ib., p. 465
133. ib., p. 466
134. 'Yet it is to be noted that the loss of chastity is irrevocable only in the upper classes. A servant or a shopkeeper's daughter may retrieve her virtue and make some honest man happy. . . . But all the Magdalens of gentle blood are tragic. . . . It is a clear case of *noblesse oblige*.' J. M. S. Tompkins, loc. cit. p. 153.
135. *M. P*, pp. 461–2
136. ib., p. 470
137. ib., p. 461
138. *Darkness and Day*
139. Leavis, II, p. 123
140. ib., p. 114
141. *Letters*, 11
142. *M. P.*, 461
143. ib., p. 250
144. *M. W.*, p. 432
145. ib., p. 437
146. ib., p. 439
147. *Letters*, 65
148. ib., 103
149. ib., 133
150. *P.*, p. 161
151. *P. P.*, p. 60. But they had attended 'morning service', in all probability.
152. *M. P.*, p. 394
153. *Some Principles of Fiction*, p. 113 and n.

EMMA

1. *Life*, p. 290
2. ib., p. 306
3. *E.*, p. xi (R.W.C.)
4. Chapman, p. 51
5. Leavis, I., pp. 75–84
6. *M. W.*, p. 314
7. Chapman, p. 50
8. *Memoir*, 2nd edit., p. 296
9. Leavis, I, p. 76
10. *M. W.*, p. 328
11. *E.*, p. 39
12. *Letters*, 86
13. ib., 89
14. ib., 141
15. *E.*, p. 197
16. ib., p. 7. But the Woodhouses evidently had their own farm; it probably pro-

duced their 'small eggs' (p. 24), and certainly the porker that they killed (p. 172).

17. *M. W.*, p. 322
18. *E.*, p. 198
19. Leavis, I, pp. 78–9
20. *E.*, p. 331
21. ib., p. 42
22. ib., p. 462
23. *P.*, p. 251
24. *E.*, pp. 260–1
25. ib., pp. 324–5
26. ib., p. 439
27. ib., p. 265
28. ib., p. 326
29. ib., p. 440
30. ib., p. 439
31. ib., p. 478
32. ib., p. 397
33. *Letters*, 18
34. *E.*, p. 240
35. *Letters*, 86
36. *P.*, pp. 98–9
37. *E.*, p. 29
38. ib., p. 62
39. ib., p. 66
40. ib., p. 64
41. ib., p. 408
42. ib., p. 66. As Donwell Abbey is 'in the parish adjoining' (p. 20), I do not quite know why Mr Knightley has so much to do with Mr Elton in his professional capacity. No doubt he also owned property in the parish of Highbury.
43. ib., p. 155
44. ib., p. 82. He might owe a few traits to Jane Austen's former admirer, Mr Blackall, that 'piece of Perfection, noisy Perfection', who was married at Clifton to a Miss Lewis (not far from Maple Grove), *Letters*, 81.
45. ib., p. 34
46. ib., p. 207
47. Chapman, p. 204
48. *E.*, p. 193
49. ib., pp. 199–200
50. ib., p. 203
51. ib., p. 204
52. ib., p. 214
53. ib., p. 219
54. ib., p. 222
55. ib., p. 227
56. ib., p. 230
57. ib., p. 240
58. ib., p. 243. This one of the few indications that Jane Fairfax appreciated "his delightful spirits".
59. ib., p. 242
60. ib., p. 243
61. ib., p. 258
62. ib., p. 260
63. ib., p. 298
64. ib., p. 316
65. ib., p. 321
66. ib., p. 12
67. ib., p. 343
68. ib., p. 345–6
69. *Some Principles of Fiction*, pp. 79–80
70. *E.*, p. 348
71. *Life*, p. 307
72. *E.*, p. 350
73. ib., p. 363
74. ib., p. 441
75. ib., p. 365
76. ib., p. 101
77. *Letters*, 139
78. *E.*, p. 369

79. ib., p. 372
80. ib., p. 373
81. ib., p. 374
82. ib., pp. 382–3
83. cf. p. 000
84. *E.*, p. 41
85. ib., p. 166
86. ib., p. 491
87. ib., p. 432
88. ib., p. 484
89. *Letters*, 76
90. *Good Behaviour* (London, 1955), p. 235
91. *E.*, p. 219
92. ib., p. 129
93. ib., p. 198
94. ib., p. 15
95. ib., p.187
96. ib., p. 214
97. ib., p.56
98. ib., p. 136. I have the impression that while members of the older aristocracy generally see exquisite refinement in Jane Austen's works, it is the recently ennobled who, well understanding the gradations of rank below them, are anxious to keep her in her middle-class place, and even to make out that she is vulgar. My generalization is based on too few instances to be worth making except in a footnote; but I recommend this line of investigation to those who have more opportunities than myself of following it up.
99. ib., p. 233
100. Leavis, I., p. 82
101. *Letters*, 103
102. *E.*, pp. 338–9
103. ib., p. 165
104. ib., pp. 300–1
105. *M. W.*, p. 318
106. *Letters*, 71
107. *Life*, p. 182
108. *E.*, p. 375
109. ib., p. 21
110. *Life of Mary Russell Mitford*, by the Rev. A. G. L'Estrange (1870) cit. *Life*, p. 300.

PERSUASION

1. *Life*, p. 333
2. ib., p. 334
3. *Letters*, 141
4. ib., 142
5. *Life*, p. 337
6. Leavis, I, p. 64
7. *The Common Reader* (first series), pp. 181–2
8. Lascelles, p. 181
9. *P.*, p. 151
10. ib., p. 154
11. ib., pp. 204–5
12. ib., p. 196
13. ib., p. 244
14. ib., p. 211
15. ib., p. 197
16. ib., p. 158. "Sir Henry Russell's widow, indeed, has no honours to distinguish her arms," says Sir Walter.

Dr Chapman conjectures that he is thinking of the *bloody hand* of Ulster, borne by baronets. But I think it just possible that the Elliots of Kellynch may have been among those baronets entitled to supporters. Supporters look particularly well on the panel of a carriage, and Sir Walter would think of them with especial complacency.

17. ib., p. 209
18. ib., p. 199
19. ib., p. 209
20. ib., p. 210
21. ib., p. 196
22. ib., p. 210
23. ib., pp. 251-2
24. ib., p. 210
25. ib., p. 104
26. ib., p. 249
27. ib., p. 199
28. ib., p. 161
29. ib., p. 5
30. ib., p. 133
31. ib., p. 215
32. ib., p. 47
33. ib., p. 249
34. ib., p. 178
35. ib., p. 135
36. ib., p. 125
37. ib., p. 11
38. ib., p. 12
39. ib., p. 16
40. ib., p. 89
41. ib., p. 28
42. ib., p. 103
43. Lascelles, p. 78
44. *P.*, pp. 50-1
45. ib., p. 64

46. Lascelles, p. 79
47. *Letters*, 70
48. *P.*, p. 68
49. *Jane Austen: a biography* (1950 edn.), p. 246. Miss Jenkins seems loath to believe that Dick was such an oaf as all that.
50. *P.*, p. 97
51. ib., p. 96
52. ib., p. 99
53. ib., p. 97
54. ib., p. 100
55. ib., p. 101
56. ib., p. 183. Dr Chapman is surely too kind (ib., p. 293) in dating Fanny Harville's death so far back as June, 1813; it was in 1814.
57. ib., p. 218. This is an opportunity to apologize for Charlotte Heywood's notorious remark in *Sanditon*: "poor Burns's known Irregularities, greatly interrupt my enjoyment of his Lines". If it were not commonly quoted in this truncated form, it would need no apology. Charlotte goes on: "I have a difficulty in depending on the *Truth* of his Feelings as a Lover. I have not faith in the *sincerity* of the affections of a Man of his description. He felt & he wrote & he forgot"(*M.W.*, p. 398). She did not so much mind him loving *sae kindly* or *sae blindly* as sae oft. Burns (who knew

that adultery *hardens all
within, and petrifies the feeling*) would humbly have
agreed with her, one ima-
gines.

58. ib., p. 109
59. Lascelles, pp. 128–9
60. *P.*, p. 85
61. *English Prose Style* (1928),
p. 119
62. Lascelles, p. 77
63. *P.*, p. 111
64. *P.*, p. 247
65. ib., p. 242
66. ib., p. 243
67. cit. Chapman, p. 98
68. ib., p. 126
69. l.c., p. 249

70. *Letters*, 103
71. *P.*, p. 28
72. ib., p. 105
73. ib., p. 124
74. ib., p. 235
75. *S. S.*, p. 38
76. *M. P.*, p. 209
77. *P.*, p. 36
78. ib., p. 84
79. ib., p. 30
80. ib., p. 233
81. *Memoir*, p. 166
82. *P.*, p. 258
83. ib., p. 240
84. ib., p. 259
85. ib., p. 263
86. ib., p. 257
87. ib., p. 258

A NOTE ON SANDITON

1. Preface to 1925 edit.
2. Chapman, pp. 208–9
3. *M. W.*, p. 403
4. ib., pp. 396–7
5. *Letters*, 116
6. *M. W.*, p. 425
7. ib., p. 363, n. 2

8. ib., p. 384
9. *E.*, p. 233
10. *P.*, p. 96
11. *M. W.*, p. 426
12. *Letters*, 142
13. *Memoir*, p. 171
14. *M. W.*, p. 381

THE LETTERS

1. *Letters*, 29
2. cit. R.W.C., Introduction to
the *Letters*
3. *Abinger Harvest*
4. ibid.
5. *Letters*, 8
6. ib., 41
7. ib., 141.1

8. ib., 142
9. ib., 10
10. ib., 6
11. ib., 2
12. ib., 7
13. ib., 17
14. ib., 130
15. ib., 66

16. ib., 102
17. ib., vii
18. ib., 28
19. ib., 30
20. ib., 32
21. ib., 29
22. *P. P.*, p. 57
23. ib., p. 364
24. *Letters*, 27

25. ib., 36
26. ib., 48
27. ib., 71
28. ib., 87
29. ib., 101
30. ib., 74.1
31. ib., 13
32. ib., 145

Index

Titles of works by Jane Austen are printed in capitals and the abbreviations used are given on page ix. The names of characters from the novels are printed in italics.

INDEX

Bennet, Mrs, 44, 45–6

Benwick, Captain, 16, 128–9, 131, 133, 134

Bertram, Edmund, 10, 27, 56, 57, 60, 64, 68; and Fanny, 65–6, 70–78, 81, 87, 110; at Sotherton, 74–6; and Lovers' Vows, 76–9

Bertram, Julia, 12, 62, 64, 69, 78–9, 84–5, 99; at Sotherton, 74–6

Bertram, Lady, 8, 62–3, 70

Bertram, Sir Thomas, 60, 63, 64, 87; and his children, 20, 68, 71, 85, 86; and Fanny, 79–82; as a letter-writer, 147, 148

Bertram, Tom, 64, 70, 71, 77, 78, 84

Bigg-Wither, Harris, 41–2, 133

Bingley, Caroline, 36, 46, 47, 51, 62

Bingley, Charles, 42, 47, 52

Blackall, Samuel, 41, 163

Blake, Charles, 91

Blake, Mrs, 91

Brandon, Colonel, 10, 16, 17, 20, 26, 31, 36

Brereton, Clara, 138, 140, 141

Bridges, Edward, 42

Brower, Reuben, 51–2

Burney, Fanny: Camilla, 4, 60; Evelina, 4, 38; Cecilia, 37–8

Burns, Robert, 165–6

Butler, Mrs John, 152

Byron, George Gordon, Lord, 129, 134, 143, 144

Campbell, Colonel, 99

Campbell, Miss, 99, 100

'Catherine, or the Bower', 1

Chapman, Dr R. W., xi, 30, 150, 154; and N. A., 1–2, 5; and P. P., 34, 35, 37; and The Watsons, 90; and E., 90, 99–100, 109; and S., 138

Churchill, Frank, 10, 92, 94–6, 97–108, 147

Churchill, Mrs, 99, 109

Clay, Mrs, 123

Coles, the, 101, 102, 105, 106, 111, 112, 113

Collins, Charlotte (née Lucas), 35, 36, 39, 42, 49–50, 53

Collins, William, 35, 37, 40, 49, 88, 97, 147; a parody of Fanny Burney, 38; and Charlotte, 49–50

Compton-Burnett, Ivy, 87

Cooke, Mr and Mrs, 88

Cooper, Rev. Edward, 40, 88, 89

Cowper, William, 14, 16, 143

Crawford, Henry, 12, 87, 94, 122; the anti-hero, 10; and Maria, 54–5, 62; and Fanny, 60, 65, 80–81, 83; his source, 61; his character, 66–73, 81, 85; at Sotherton, 74–6; and Lovers' Vows, 77–9

Crawford, Mary, 61, 64, 65, 87, 89, 94, 123, 147, 149; and Edmund, 57–8, 81; her character, 67–73, 161; at Sotherton, 74–6; and Lovers' Vows, 77–9

Croft, Admiral and Mrs, 94, 119, 126, 130, 136–7

Darcy, Fitzwilliam, 10, 36, 38, 43–4, 66, 93, 94; and Elizabeth Bennet, 45, 51–3

Darcy, George, 54

Darcy, Georgiana, 37, 94

Dashwood, Elinor, 15, 18, 20, 31, 157; her self-command, 17, 21, 24–5; and Willoughby, 26, 31–2; her marriage of sensibility, 26; and Lucy Steele, 27–8, 29; compared with Elizabeth Bennet, 36–7

Dashwood, Fanny, 23, 27, 30, 32

Dashwood, John, 15, 23, 32, 37

Dashwood, Mrs John, 15, 21, 25, 27, 30, 32

Dashwood, Margaret, 25, 32–3

Dashwood, Marianne, xii, 32, 42, 94, 157; her sensibility, 14, 16–17, 21, 24, 134; and Willoughby, 15, 18–20, 26, 31; her predisposition to romance, 17–20, 22; her lack of candour, 21–3, 87; her conversion, 23, 41, 44; and money, 25–7; compared with Jane Bennet, 36–7

INDEX

INDEX